INTEGRATING RESEARCH AND EDUCATION

BIOCOMPLEXITY INVESTIGATORS EXPLORE THE POSSIBILITIES

SUMMARY OF A WORKSHOP

Bridget K. B. Avila

Board on Life Sciences
Division on Earth and Life Studies

NATIONAL RESEARCH COUNCIL
OF THE NATIONAL ACADEMIES

THE NATIONAL ACADEMIES PRESS
Washington, D.C.
www.nap.edu

THE NATIONAL ACADEMIES PRESS 500 Fifth Street, N.W. Washington, DC 20001

NOTICE: The project that is the subject of this report was approved by the Governing Board of the National Research Council, whose members are drawn from the councils of the National Academy of Sciences, the National Academy of Engineering, and the Institute of Medicine. The members of the planning group responsible for the report were chosen for their special competences and with regard for appropriate balance.

This study was supported by agreement DUE-0126403 between the National Academies and the National Science Foundation. Any opinions, findings, conclusions, or recommendations expressed in this publication do not necessarily reflect the views of the organizations or agencies that provided support for the project.

International Standard Book Number 0-309-08871-2 (Book)
International Standard Book Number 0-309-50622-0 (PDF)

Additional copies of this report are available from the National Academies Press, 500 Fifth Street, NW, Lockbox 285, Washington, DC 20055; (800) 624-6242 or (202) 334-3313 (in the Washington metropolitan area); Internet, http://www.nap.edu

Printed in the United States of America.

THE NATIONAL ACADEMIES

Advisers to the Nation on Science, Engineering, and Medicine

The **National Academy of Sciences** is a private, nonprofit, self-perpetuating society of distinguished scholars engaged in scientific and engineering research, dedicated to the furtherance of science and technology and to their use for the general welfare. Upon the authority of the charter granted to it by the Congress in 1863, the Academy has a mandate that requires it to advise the federal government on scientific and technical matters. Dr. Bruce M. Alberts is president of the National Academy of Sciences.

The **National Academy of Engineering** was established in 1964, under the charter of the National Academy of Sciences, as a parallel organization of outstanding engineers. It is autonomous in its administration and in the selection of its members, sharing with the National Academy of Sciences the responsibility for advising the federal government. The National Academy of Engineering also sponsors engineering programs aimed at meeting national needs, encourages education and research, and recognizes the superior achievements of engineers. Dr. Wm. A. Wulf is president of the National Academy of Engineering.

The **Institute of Medicine** was established in 1970 by the National Academy of Sciences to secure the services of eminent members of appropriate professions in the examination of policy matters pertaining to the health of the public. The Institute acts under the responsibility given to the National Academy of Sciences by its congressional charter to be an adviser to the federal government and, upon its own initiative, to identify issues of medical care, research, and education. Dr. Harvey V. Fineberg is president of the Institute of Medicine.

The **National Research Council** was organized by the National Academy of Sciences in 1916 to associate the broad community of science and technology with the Academy's purposes of furthering knowledge and advising the federal government. Functioning in accordance with general policies determined by the Academy, the Council has become the principal operating agency of both the National Academy of Sciences and the National Academy of Engineering in providing services to the government, the public, and the scientific and engineering communities. The Council is administered jointly by both Academies and the Institute of Medicine. Dr. Bruce M. Alberts and Dr. Wm. A. Wulf are chair and vice chair, respectively, of the National Research Council.

www.national-academies.org

PLANNING GROUP FOR THE WORKSHOP ON INTEGRATING EDUCATION IN BIOCOMPLEXITY RESEARCH

LOUIS GROSS (Chair), University of Tennessee, Knoxville, Tennessee
CAROL BREWER, University of Montana, Missoula, Montana
DIANE EBERT-MAY, Michigan State University, East Lansing, Michigan
DAVID MOGK, Montana State University, Bozeman, Montana
JOAN B. ROSE, Michigan State University, East Lansing, Michigan

Staff

KERRY A. BRENNER, Study Director, Board on Life Sciences
JAY B. LABOV, Deputy Director, Center for Education
VALERIE GUTMANN, Project Assistant, Board on Life Sciences
NORMAN GROSSBLATT, Senior Editor, Division on Earth and Life Studies

Preface

In recent years, the National Science Foundation (NSF) has been working to develop closer links between the funding of scientific research and increasing public understanding of science. Its efforts to improve public understanding of science have focused on schools, colleges, and universities but have included support for museums, aquariums, and other programs. Those efforts are designed to prepare future scientists and educators, as well as to inform the public about how science affects society. One mechanism that NSF is using to connect education and outreach efforts to scientific research is the addition of "Criterion 2" (see below) to NSF grant proposals (*http://www.nsf.gov/od/opp/opp_advisory/oaccrit2.htm*):

Criterion 1: What is the intellectual merit of the proposed activity?
Criterion 2: What are the broader impacts of the proposed activity?

NSF has asked that grant writers consider the following questions, related to Criterion 2, as they prepare their proposals.

- What are the broader impacts of the proposed activity?
- How well does the activity advance discovery and understanding while promoting teaching, training and learning?"
- How well does the proposed activity broaden the participation of underrepresented groups (for example, ethnic minorities)?"
- To what extent will it enhance the infrastructure for research and education, such as facilities, instrumentation, networks, and partnerships?

- Will the results be disseminated broadly to enhance scientific and technologic understanding?
- What are the expected benefits of the activity to society?

Those charged with reviewing grant proposals are asked to consider the impact and feasibility of proposed activities in making funding decisions. To satisfy Criterion 2, most research grant proposals now choose to describe planned education or outreach activities and how they are related to the proposed research. These activities may involve formal education in schools, colleges, and universities; outreach via public seminars and journalism; or activities in museums and aquariums.

NSF's Biocomplexity in the Environment initiative has been one of the few programs to require that applicants explicitly include an education or outreach component. This initiative has already gone through three funding cycles. Reviews of grant proposals and progress reports showed that many of the early education and outreach projects had not been as carefully planned as the research proposed. Many were too ambitious given the time and expertise available, others were limited in scope and would impact only a few students. NSF concluded that the proposals might improve if grant applicants became more familiar with existing high-quality projects in education and outreach. Outreach is no easy task, but successful models can make the goal of designing new programs much easier and those who are aware of the models are more likely to avoid the common pitfalls. It therefore asked the National Research Council to organize a Workshop on Integrating Education in Biocomplexity Research to bring together scientists with biocomplexity-related grants and scientists involved in designing, managing, or evaluating education and outreach activities.

The workshop was held on April 15-16, 2002. A planning group arranged the workshop, identified topics and speakers, and developed the agenda but did not participate in the writing of this summary. The author of the summary is Bridget K.B. Avila, who was not a member of the planning group.

This summary was prepared to synthesize the ideas that emerged from the gathering and to provide additional guidance to scientists on communicating the broader context of their work to students, teachers, and the general public.

Acknowledgments

This workshop summary was enhanced by the contributions of many individuals who graciously offered their time, expertise, and knowledge. The planning group thanks all who attended and/or participated in the workshop (see Appendix B for biographies of planning group and workshop speakers).

This summary has been reviewed in draft form by individuals chosen for their diverse perspectives and technical expertise, in accordance with procedures approved by the National Research Council's Report Review Committee. The purpose of this independent review is to provide candid and critical comments that will assist the institution in making its published summary as sound as possible and to ensure that the summary meets institutional standards for objectivity, evidence, and responsiveness to the study charge. The review comments and draft manuscript remain confidential. We thank the following individuals for their review of this summary:

Juliann Allison, University of California, Riverside
Alan Berkowitz, Institute for Environmental Modeling
Mary Colvard, New York State Department of Education
Diane Ebert-May, Michigan State University
Louis Gross, University of Tennessee
Richard Norgaard, University of California, Berkeley

Although the reviewers listed above have provided constructive comments and suggestions, they did not see the final draft of the report before its release. The review of this summary was overseen by Robert R. Sokal of the State University of New York at Stony Brook. Appointed by the National Research Council, he was responsible for making certain that an independent examination of this summary was carried out in accordance with institutional procedures and that all review comments were carefully considered. Responsibility for the final content of this summary rests entirely with the institution.

Contents

APPENDIXES

Introduction

Principal investigators of natural science research projects are accustomed to designing fresh approaches to research problems, but most face a formidable challenge when attempting to integrate education into their research. Many find that they are not sufficiently cognizant of modern educational methods to appropriately inform either the general student population or the general public about their science. Likewise, many educators strive to communicate the excitement and importance of science to students and the public, but do not always have access to information on the latest research advances.

THE WORKSHOP

The National Science Foundation (NSF) proposed a National Research Council workshop as a way to help researchers to incorporate effective educational components into their research proposals. The goals were to help principal investigators to design educational endeavors that would broaden the impact of science and to foster collaboration and communication among researchers and educators. The invitees were in three categories: members of teams that had already received large grants for biocomplexity research projects, those who had received "incubation grants" that would enable them to develop full research proposals in the future, and science educators invited to help lead discussions.

In designing the workshop, the planning group wanted to emphasize the dynamics of combining education and research: helping students to acquire scientific habits of mind, translating discoveries into instructional resources, brokering collaborations, and attracting larger numbers and more diverse populations of students to continue studying the sciences. Thus, the group's intentions when designing the workshop were to provide the attendees with an initial community-building atmosphere and to provide material for a summary that could serve as a useful guide for both educators and scientists in any field. The planning group set out to inform the workshop participants about the many methods that can be used to meet educational goals and about how to design education projects compatible with their research and expertise.

The workshop included case-study discussions in small groups and larger group activities accompanied by discussion. The format was chosen as a way to demonstrate and model effective ways to communicate information and trigger learning. For example, at the beginning of the workshop Lou Gross encouraged participants to interact in small groups by leading them in an activity called the "polya-urn experiment," which he used as an example of a simple manipulative experiment that can generate complex, nonintuitive results. Dr. Gross has used this experiment in groups from elementary school to graduate school, with learning objectives differing with level of experience. (See box.)

Diane Ebert-May later engaged the audience in a survey that used small Post-it notes to build bar graphs of participant responses to questions. Throughout the workshop audience members were encouraged to gather in small groups to discuss their reactions to presentations. All of these approaches served to model a variety of educational activities available beyond the formal lecture.

The scientific theme of the workshop was biocomplexity. NSF defines biocomplexity as referring to "the dynamic web of often surprising interrelationships that arise when components of the global ecosystem—biological, physical, chemical, and the human dimension—interact. Investigations of Biocomplexity in the Environment are intended to provide a more complete understanding of natural processes, of human behaviors and decisions in the natural world, and of ways to use new technology effectively to observe the environment and sustain the diversity of life on Earth" (*http://www.nsf.gov/pubs/2001/nsf0134/nsf0134.htm*). Rita Colwell, director of NSF, further explained, "Biocomplexity is understanding how the components of a global system interact with the biological, physical, chemical, and human dimension, all taken together to gain an understanding of the

Polya-Urn Experiment

The participants were broken into groups of three to four individuals, and each group carried out experiments by drawing beads of two different colors from an urn. Starting with two beads in each urn, one person of each group drew a bead at random (without looking) and replaced it, another person noted which color bead was drawn, while yet another member of the group then added another bead of the same color as the one drawn to the urn. The urn was shaken and the process repeated many times.

One can think of each urn as an island with one individual of each of two species, each of which is equally likely to reproduce (asexually) in one time period. At the end of the game each group counted the number of beads of each color in the urn and compared the results of the experiments done by the other groups. As a group continues to play the game the fraction of beads of one color in any one urn approaches a limit, but the fractions will not be the same in each urn. It can be proven that the fraction approached within an urn has a limit distribution that is uniformly distributed between 0 and 1.

(For more on this subject, see Cohen, Joel E. 1976. Irreproducible Results and the Breeding of Pigs (or Nondegenerate Limit Random Variables in Biology). BioScience 26:391-394.

complexity of the system and to be able to derive fundamental principles from it. I personally think we'll be able to have a scientific understanding of sustainability even perhaps a series of formulae or equations, developed by mathematicians to explain and define sustainability. We'll be able to develop a predictive capacity for actions taken with respect to the environment to predict specific outcomes. We can't do this yet well, we can predict, but it's not precise and quantitative. After investing in biocomplexity research, we'll be able to make predictions concerning environmental phenomena as a consequence of human actions taken." [1]

---

[1]An Interview with Rita Colwell, *Scientist* 14(19):0, Oct. 2, 2000 (*http://www.the-scientist.com/yr2000/oct/emmett_p0_001002.html*)

The speakers and other participants share an interest in studying connections within the global ecosystem. They do not all interpret biocomplexity in the same way, but they generally agree that the study of biocomplexity can enhance our understanding of our world. Research findings in biocomplexity are appropriate for conveying science to students and the general public because they often involve issues in the public sphere. The topic was chosen as a model for the workshop in the hope that it will be helpful to researchers in other fields striving toward the goals suggested in Criterion 2.

PRODUCTS OF THE WORKSHOP

The products of the workshop are this summary and a Web site *(http://dlesecommunity.carleton.edu/biocomplexity/)* that contains links to currently funded biocomplexity projects, to Web resources that support biocomplexity research, and to tips on partnering, assessment, and dissemination. The site also has spaces for discussion groups and for posting available resources.

This summary is written for both principal investigators (who are commonly also educators) and educators (who many times do research) to give them a sense of important issues to consider in designing scientific education and outreach projects. The workshop addressed, and this summary presents, a wide array of ideas for investigators and educators who are considering how to respond to the challenges of Criterion 2. The ideas presented here are certainly not exhaustive of all possibilities for integrating research and education, but they should provide readers with a foundation for approaching the design and implementation of education components of research projects.

Many attendees at the Workshop on Integrating Education in Biocomplexity Research supported the idea of collaborating with others who have complementary expertise to create and run education and outreach projects. The idea behind such partnerships is that education would benefit in the same way that interdisciplinary scientific studies benefit from research collaboration. The goal of the partnerships would be a combination of the talents of principal investigators and educators to communicate the results of research more effectively to varied audiences (schoolchildren, museum visitors, science journalists [and their readers], policy-makers, and so on).

Summary of the Workshop

In his introductory remarks, Louis Gross (University of Tennessee), chair of the workshop planning group, explained what he and the group saw as the different ways to interpret the workshop title, "Integrating Education in Biocomplexity Research." The group chose that title because of its multiple meanings, recognizing the benefits of approaching the workshop from several viewpoints. One view is that a larger audience would be educated about the science of biocomplexity, another is that biocomplexity researchers themselves would learn about approaches to educational research. Mechanisms for communicating with students and the public about biocomplexity can be enhanced by education research. Gross emphasized the wealth of knowledge that educators have to offer scientists. The field of education has its own research community, and principal investigators (many of whom also consider themselves educators) can tap into that research to learn how people learn about science—for example, the findings of research on learning (see Appendix E).

Throughout the workshop, examples of how research and education might be integrated were highlighted. Seven case studies and several hypothetical scenarios were discussed, including scenarios of how researchers might develop education projects directed toward target audiences, such as postdoctoral researchers, graduate and undergraduate students, K-12 students and educators, students in professional programs (law, medicine, journalism, and so on), policy-makers, nonscience professionals, and people associated with the informal education community (museums, aquariums,

Outline of Ideas and Themes Generated During the Workshop

1. Collaborating with others with complementary talents is potentially quite valuable, but requires mutual benefits that exceed costs or the benefits of working alone, and requires careful facilitation, logistics and modeling.
    a. Researchers can benefit from the knowledge educators have to offer (e.g., the American Association for the Advancement of Science education materials, education researchers).
    b. If researchers are going to contribute to teaching, they need to understand teachers' constraints, use mutually respectful language, share work equitably, etc.
2. Scientists and those they might collaborate with through education share many things in common.
    a. Teachers and scientists share a passion for learning. They both must deal with a public that sometimes follows them with blind faith, and at other times questions their motives.
    b. Journalists and scientists share curiosity laced with skepticism and need to see evidence, a belief that the truth exists and that it is imperative to find and communicate it.
    c. Education researchers, assessment specialists, and scientists share a focus on questions, hypotheses, careful methods, peer review, etc.

and so on). According to NSF guidelines, researchers need not limit themselves to universities or even educational institutions in complying with Criterion 2, but can reach out to all parts of society—science affects everyone.

Several presenters of case studies and some planning group members offered suggestions for integrating education and research drawn from their specific experiences. Their suggestions were based on extensive experience with education projects. The projects themselves are described here as case studies, and several are treated in Appendix D, which presents information on evaluation and assessment. Most of the case studies describe projects targeted to particular audiences (such as undergraduates or museum visi-

3. As a corollary to integrating education into research, we can work to integrate research into the education work we do. This was highlighted by the comments of Keesing, Levitan, and Ebert-May.
4. Involving nonscientists in research is a means of providing valuable professional development opportunities, e.g., for teachers (Carvellas) and journalists (Kastens), as well as for future scientists (Manduca). Clear guidelines exist for designing such research experiences, at least for young scientists (Manduca) and teachers (Carvellas).
5. Undergraduate curriculum reform, such as the University of Michigan example, might be one of the most logical ways of linking research and education but numerous barriers exist to giving such efforts the time, collaboration, and attention required. Indeed, one would think that the undergraduate arena should be the first place to look for ways of infusing the latest research into teaching, creating models for application in other arenas.
6. There is a useful multiplier effect from working with the teachers of teachers or journalists (e.g., Kastens).
7. It is imperative to have the same high standard of excellence for the education component as for the research component. Allowing education work to be voluntary for researchers was seen as essential for achieving this goal, at least at one of the institutions highlighted in the workshop summary (Woods Hole Oceanographic Institution).
8. Assessment and evaluation are imperative in considering the effectiveness of an educational component of a project.

tors), but many of the comments will be helpful when applied to other groups. The box above provides an outline of important ideas and themes explored during the workshop.

PRINCIPLES OF RESEARCH APPLIED TO EDUCATION PROJECTS

Herb Levitan, of the NSF Division of Undergraduate Education, asked workshop attendees to think of education projects with a perspective that parallels that of scientific research. He began by asking the attendees to indicate what they believe are the core principles of research. Attendees discussed their ideas in small groups and then offered their answers to the audience at large. Themes of various principles among the attendees' responses included the joy of discovery, working with others, breaking down disciplinary walls, integrity and rigor of research, and sharing the scientific experience with students.

Levitan proposed, in line with what the attendees had identified as essential principles of research, that there are four principles that guide research, and that these principles should also be applied to projects that integrate education and research. He proposed that these efforts should

- *Be original and break new ground.* The best research is that which builds on the efforts of others, explores unknown territory, and risks failure.
- *Provide opportunities for professional development.* Research provides opportunities for personal growth for all who are actively involved. More-experienced researchers may act as mentors or trainers of those with less experience—the "learners." Learners gain confidence and stature among peers as they gain proficiency in a field.
- *Provide opportunities for collaboration and cooperation.* Because the most interesting and important problems and questions are usually complex and multidisciplinary, researchers with diverse and complementary perspectives and experiences often collaborate.
- *Provide opportunities for work that results in a product.* The expectation of all research is that the outcomes will be communicated and available to an audience beyond those immediately involved in the research activity. That can occur via peer-reviewed publication or via patents or commercial products. The value of the research will then be measured by the impact of its product—how widely cited or otherwise used it is.

GETTING STARTED FORMING COLLABORATIONS

Cathryn Manduca, of Carleton College, gave advice based on her experiences with the Keck Geology Consortium. "While collaboration is regarded as a valuable experience, it is also a costly one. It takes time. It takes money. It takes a strong base of communication. To be worthwhile, a collaboration should take place only when working together as a group is better than working alone as individuals."

In her keynote address to workshop attendees, Patricia Morse, of the University of Washington, echoed Manduca's advice that collaborations should be formed only when they will yield more to the participants than would acting alone and noted that the needs of all parties in the collaboration must be considered. "Both sides have expectations that need to be thoroughly considered." Morse also offered guiding principles to consider when forming a collaboration. In order to achieve quality outcomes, she advised that collaborators should "be very careful to choose high-quality participants with strong backgrounds."

According to Morse, one way to foster collaborations across expertise lines would be to "include experts from the field of education in meetings geared toward principal investigators and connect the relevant principal investigators with each other. For example, someone working with butterflies could approach NSF to get connected with other researchers in a specific field." Morse concluded, "Successful collaborations should be celebrated, and participants in a collaboration should be given time to reflect on their experiences and possibly work with their project mentors to plan their next steps."

Morse also cautioned against harboring common misconceptions regarding education and research. She noted three misconceptions in particular, first that teaching is intuitive, or that instructors often assume that the way they learned is *the* way to learn. This attitude ignores the wealth of research in cognitive sciences. Secondly, she noted the misconception that undergraduates can't do research, despite the fact that some scientists' best work is done at a very early age. The third misconception she noted was that scientists can't understand "education-ese," or that they don't have time to learn about what education experts have to offer. She suggested that avoiding these misconceptions and instead looking toward solutions would aid collaborators in their efforts to integrate research and education.

Susan Singer, of Carleton College, suggested that a collaboration should be considered as something that does not necessarily revolve around the principal investigator. "Those who are interested in collaborations should consider research projects with both undergraduate science students and education students, that is, being partners in the education process and creating a culture that encourages an exchange of ideas about teaching that parallels the culture of exchange of ideas dealing with our own research. This type of exchange deals with professional development, so education and research are fully integrated."

John Farrington, of the Woods Hole Oceanographic Institution, offered ideas for facilitating relationships in a collaboration based on his experiences at Woods Hole. One such approach that is now under way is what Farrington called a reverse workshop, in which teachers educate scientists and those involved in informal education. To design such a workshop, one could have master teachers, informal educators, or cognitive psychologists teach scientists about curriculum standards, expectations, or advances in research on how people learn. Additionally, senior faculty or research scholars who have some experience in collaborative efforts between scientists and educators can act as mentors in such programs.

Farrington emphasized the need for openness and patience in forming a collaboration. "Keep diversity needs in mind throughout the process, programs, and activities. Maintain patience and persistence leavened with appropriately aggressive goals and approaches."

Angelo Collins, of the Knowles Science Teaching Foundation, noted the importance of logistics in forming a collaboration. Logistics can be one of the most serious problems: time, place or distance, and expense can cause unnecessary hurdles in a project.

Collins explained that education and science have different cultures and that part of what a school-science partnership attempts is to create a new culture that is a blend of the two. "It is a point to keep in mind that scientists have more resources and status than teachers. But even more pressing in the age of standards testing is the level of accountability that teachers face. An analogous situation for principal investigators might be if the local newspaper published on the front page, not their research grant or publications, but the number of citations of their publications, something over which they have no control—and if, on the basis of those data, it were decided whether they would get salary increases, stay in their departments, or keep their jobs at all. That kind of accountability is what teachers are facing, and it would be smart to keep this in mind in forming a partnership."

Collins suggested that teachers and scientists working together must pay attention to who talks and who listens and who is doing the routine work. To show respect for one another, it is important to have an equitable distribution of both ideas and work assignments. One workshop participant likened such understanding of cultural differences to the same kind of understanding that would be needed at a stakeholders' meeting—one can't assume that the same tacit knowledge is shared by all. Collins encouraged celebration among collaborators—they should look on informal social gatherings as necessary for forming bonds that facilitate working together.

Patricia Morse suggested that collaborators share leadership duties and responsibilities. She mentioned her experience that anyone given the appropriate resources can function as a leader if there are shared values among the members of a community (or collaboration). This type of behavior is very different from the common hierarchical structure of the university.

CONSIDERING A TARGET AUDIENCE

In considering how to engage members of the public in an understanding of science, Kastens suggested that "researchers ask themselves why they think that the public should care about their research. Questions can be asked of people in specific situations to identify the kinds of information that will be important to them. Why would a researcher want various kinds of people to know about his or her work, and what details would they want him or him to know? A voter? A parent shopping for a family's groceries? Property developers? An elderly person newly diagnosed with cancer? A Senate staffer? Any of those could be part of a target audience, and education projects aimed at them would be different from one another."

Manduca pointed out that the target audience of a project must also be considered in the dissemination of the project results. "Results should be communicated with the intended audience in mind and how that audience might receive the results—in written form, via the Internet, or by some other means."

Students in other professional programs would benefit from exposure to science, and providing in-depth experiences with science before graduation can provide a useful background to students going into teaching, law, medicine, or even the clergy. Teachers are a relatively well-understood constituency for integrating research and education, but other professions would be worthy of attention from principal investigators. An attorney with research experience in environmental science will make a better environmental lawyer. A physician with knowledge of environmental impacts on health will view his or her practice of medicine more broadly. Clergy with exposure to biomedical science and research will make better-informed spiritual leaders. As one workshop participant noted, elected officials often have a frighteningly limited understanding of controversial issues involving scientific knowledge. An increased exposure to science would result in better-informed public officials to the benefit of their constituencies.

Case Study 1
Cathryn Manduca, Carleton College—Designing Research Experiences for Undergraduates

The Keck Geology Consortium involves the coordination of students and faculty from the 12 member institutions in a four-week summer research experience. The W.M. Keck Foundation, the National Science Foundation, the Exxon Educational Foundation, the American Association of Petroleum Geologists Foundation, and 12 liberal-arts member institutions fund the consortium. The consortium is a group of small geoscience departments in predominantly undergraduate, liberal-arts institutions that cooperate to improve geoscience education through research. The primary activity of the consortium is to sponsor projects involving faculty and undergraduate students in a collaborative effort to solve geoscience problems. For more information about the consortium, see *http://keck.carleton.edu/.*

The overall structure of the consortium involves matching three faculty members with nine students. Over 4 weeks in the summer, students work together in groups on several projects in a variety of subjects and design individual projects for themselves. By the end of the summer experience, students are expected to have the necessary data from their projects to look at a scientific question in depth. Their results are discussed with an on-campus mentor from the Consortium who works collaboratively with faculty members from other institutions. This format allows students to experience a

WHAT CONSTITUTES AN EFFECTIVE UNDERGRADUATE RESEARCH PROJECT?

In designing an educational component and integrating it into an undergraduate research initiative, one of the first steps is to identify the elements needed for a successful project. Manduca offered detailed advice on forming and implementing an education or outreach project on the basis of her experience with the Keck Geology Consortium (see Case Study 1). According to Manduca, the first step in designing an undergraduate research experience must be clear delineation of the goals of the program. Once the goals are understood and embraced, decisions about how to design the educational experience will flow naturally from the goal. Manduca outlined the Keck Geology Consortium's two main sets of goals (one for student education, and the other for faculty professional development).

breadth of topics and a depth of knowledge in a particular subject. At the end of the academic year, students present their results at an annual symposium, which may be held at their own academic institution or some other site.

"Within the overall framework, faculty members are free to design group projects with any structure they think would best serve their interests," Manduca noted. "Students who have gone through the consortium experience have given witness to its impact on them. They have reported gaining an understanding of scientific inquiry; in-depth, integrated, self-directed learning in their field of interest; technical, interpersonal, and communication skills valued by graduate schools and employers; and a test of their career interests. As one student reported, 'This experience is unparalleled by anything else I have ever done.'"

The impact on faculty can also be tremendous. Faculty members report gaining resources and ideas for teaching, increased content knowledge, and new research interests and techniques.

Note: The Keck Geology Consortium is funded by the W.M. Keck Foundation, NSF, Exxon Educational Foundation, American Association of Petroleum Geologists Foundation, and 12 liberal-arts member institutions (Amherst College, Beloit College, Carleton College, Colorado College, Franklin & Marshall College, Pomona College, Smith College, Trinity University, Washington and Lee University, Whitman College, Williams College, and the College of Wooster).

Student Education:

• *Help students to develop intellectual, technical, and personal skills.* The research experience should enhance students' intellectual growth and give them technical and personal skills that they would not have developed otherwise.

• *Encourage and test career interests.* Give students a variety of opportunities to experience work in a field so that they can determine whether they want to pursue further study or a career in that field.

Faculty Professional Development:

• *Encourage interactions.* Interactions could be among faculty from different institutions. This can be especially helpful for researchers working in small departments in small institutions whose opportunities for such interactions might otherwise be few.

- *Enhance research.* This usually means ultimately generating results that are published.

In defining an expanded set of goals for a research experience, one should consider the needs of all stakeholders—students, faculty, the institution, and so on. Institutional goals may include building connections to industry or other universities or otherwise gaining exposure that might not be possible without a collaborative relationship.

Constraints will always need to be considered in designing a project, just as there are constraints in designing an experiment to test a particular hypothesis. Manduca suggested that in both, one must first identify the goals of the project. The consortium faculty wanted their students to

- Do science—from project design to public presentation of results.
- Study a problem in detail.
- Learn specific research techniques.
- Develop and experience the empowerment that comes from collaboration, writing, and speaking skills.
- Gain confidence, both personally and as researchers.
- Test career interests.

Manduca reported that when students in the consortium were asked what their goals were, they named goals similar to those laid out by the faculty described above. Undergraduate students wanted to

- Do science in a particular subdiscipline (to test career and intellectual interests).
- Apply classroom learning to work on a real problem.
- Gain job skills or graduate-school credentials.
- Work in groups.
- Gain confidence.

Manduca defined four steps of designing student research experiences, each with its own set of issues or concerns as follows.

1. Define the Problem

The issues involved in this step constitute an overview of the entire research plan: ensuring student ownership of a problem; finding a meaningful and well-defined problem; finding a project that can be done within the constraints of time, equipment, logistics, and funding; aligning the problem with laboratory priorities and research plans; and discerning the level of knowledge and preparation that students bring to the research experience.

Manduca and various participants identified strategies to help students to address those issues:

- Guiding them through the research literature and mentoring them in developing a project that suits their interests.
- Introducing a problem and then helping them to choose from a list of possible projects.
- Allowing the whole group to collaborate in choosing projects.
- Assigning a project to a student according to the student's knowledge and expertise level.

2. Develop the Research Plan

Manduca put forth several questions for research students to consider at this step in the development of their project: Will planned experiments respond to the hypothesis? Is the project feasible with respect to time, equipment, and personnel costs? Can the students learn the necessary techniques and interpret the results? Does their plan address goals established by faculty and students? Does the plan maximize the experience for all of the students?

One strategy for developing the students' research plan includes the proposal writing and review cycle (with students acting as peer reviewers for each other). In some cases, it may work best for students to develop plans that incorporate faculty-defined standard protocols for data collection and analysis.

3. Collect and Interpret Data

According to Manduca, issues to consider with respect to students' collecting and interpreting data include the identification of meaningless data early so that the experimental design can be redirected. Other potential issues include technical glitches or problems with laboratory schedules, time management, support vs. independence of students, and responsibilities to sponsors. Possible strategies to address these problems are one-on-one mentoring, peer mentoring or mentoring within research teams, and structured reporting or checkpoints.

4. Communicate the Results

Manduca suggested that faculty must consider how to foster a successful quality presentation by the students. Important considerations include providing a meaningful venue for presentations and setting up a mechanism for the review and critique of students' research results. Possible strategies include group presentations on campus or at national research fairs or professional society meetings, community presentations, Internet discussion groups, and papers that are reviewed by other students or scientists.

Manduca underscored that faculty at liberal-arts colleges do research with undergraduates more frequently than their colleagues at major research universities. "Someone at a large university who is considering developing a research experience for undergraduates should consider collaborating with a faculty member at a liberal-arts college."

Many of the issues outlined by Manduca about what constitutes an effective undergraduate research experience are issues that may be faced when developing a course or set of courses for undergraduates. Ben van der Pluijm, of the University of Michigan, presented a case study (Case Study 2) on an interdisciplinary undergraduate program at his institution that paralleled many of Manduca's points. Many of these issues could be considered universal to the goal of integrating research and education as they deal with educating both a larger audience about a particular area of science and science researchers themselves learning about effective educational approaches.

Felicia Keesing of Bard College presented a case study (see Case Study 3) that considered integrating research and education more from the point of view of educational research. This epistemological view is yet another approach for working with undergraduates or any other type of knowledge recipient.

Case Study 2
Ben van der Pluijm, University of Michigan Global Change Program

The University of Michigan's Global Change Program (*http://www.globalchange.umich.edu/*) offers an interdisciplinary approach to undergraduate science and social-science education as part of the university's Program in the Environment. In three interdisciplinary, team-taught courses, the topics of global change are examined from physical and human perspectives, and case studies are used to explore conditions for sustainability.

The courses are aimed at first- and second-year students who want to understand historical and modern aspects of global change. These 4-credit courses include hands-on sections. A minor in global change can be completed in the first few years of study; the three global change courses are its required core and students learn further through the completion of two elective, campus-wide courses.

The objective of this program is to help students to understand and participate in the debate on global environmental change. Students take a series of interdisciplinary courses over three semesters. The curriculum consists of three possible tracks for students to pursue: natural sciences, social sciences, and sustainability studies. Learning goals in the curriculum include

- Understanding of the underpinnings of science.
- Understanding scales of change.
- Understanding how human actions affect the environment.
- Helping students to become more informed citizens and decision-makers through the application of evidence.
- Applying interdisciplinary approaches to problems.

Such an extensive effort will likely include administrative hurdles. "Faculty involved in the program created a grass-roots movement to get the program operating despite the university," as van der Pluijm put it. The faculty members engaged in the program have put forth a great deal of time and effort and are enriched by this extra effort. The faculty focuses on the linkages between the natural and social sciences with the aim of a seamless integration of materials. Learning is active for students in the program, who use multimedia tools and hands-on experiences throughout their coursework. Interdisciplinary courses are most often deferred until later in the average undergraduate career, but laboratory work in the Global Change Program (whose students are often first- or second-year students) is interdisciplinary from the start, focusing on such problems as predicting changes in climate with CO_2 datasets (though some workshop participants suggested that interdisciplinary courses aren't always ideal for students at the beginning of their academic careers). In their first semester, students study physical processes. In the second semester, van der Pluijm reports, "a focus is placed on human impacts of global change, although instructors are careful not to stress the severity of the situation, so as not to discourage students to the point where they lose interest in the class." In the third semester, students do capstone work involving a variety of fields—sustainability studies, analyzing different countries' demographics, colonial history, climate-change policies, public health, and natural resources.

Students may minor in the program, and this minor is recognized in many schools in the university. Support and analysis of the program are provided by both the National Science Foundation and the university's School of Education. Courses are managed via a Web environment (interactive, frequently updated Web pages with notes, syllabus information, and announcements) and e-mail. Grade feedback (rank in class, and so on) is provided throughout each course, and students are able to evaluate instructors and topics throughout the semester so that necessary changes in course design can be implemented as soon as possible. Exit and graduate interviews are also used as evaluation tools for the program, and these tools are continually under development. (See Appendix D for an evaluation of this program.)

WORKING WITH K-12 EDUCATORS

Several presenters at the workshop are involved in K-12 science-education projects. Monica Elser, of Arizona State University (see Case Study 4), led the audience in a discussion on how they perceived the challenges and benefits of scientists and K-12 teachers working together. Investigators in other fields could use these lists as a means to provoke thinking about how scientists and teachers could best work together.

Potential benefits for scientists:
- Learning new teaching methods.
- Thinking more broadly and deeply about the learning process.

Potential challenges for scientists:

Case Study 3
Felicia Keesing, Bard College—Integrating Research and Education—An Epistemologic View of How the Scientific Method Can Aid Learning

As an assistant professor at Bard College, Felicia Keesing has studied how students learn and is conducting an experiment to demonstrate the effects of first-hand involvement in research on how students perceive knowledge.

Keesing hypothesizes that higher-order thinking skills might be influenced in a positive way by scientific research, so her research focuses on epistemology. Epistemology is the study of how a person knows something or what someone believes knowledge to be or what knowledge is. If one of the main goals of education is for students to develop critical thinking skills, then epistemology is essential to education. One can begin thinking of how epistemology folds into teaching by proposing different questions about knowledge: Is knowledge about a topic something that is given by an authority figure? Is knowledge about a topic something that is absolute and unchanging?

Some studies have demonstrated that alternative educational approaches can influence the rate of development through levels of epistemologic development. One such study showed that a one-semester experience can influence the rate of epistemologic development of students. The study included two control groups and one experimental group, each consisting of about 25 students. All three groups were enrolled in a course on environmental issues. The control groups took the class in a standard lecture format; the experimental group's class was designed specifically to increase the rate of their epistemologic development. The experimental class focused on controversial environmental issues, such as air or water pollution, nuclear power, and toxic-waste disposal. Students were assigned to study multiple sides of those issues and to write and discuss their perspectives. The course ended with some questions unanswered.

"Pushing students into more challenging work and learning processes than lecture formats to which they were more likely accustomed is an approach common in the educational literature on epistemologic development," Keesing explained. "It follows a guiding rule known as the 'plus-one rule and disequilibrium.' This rule states that in order to influence the development rate of students, an educator should target their activities about one stage beyond where they are to create a disequilibrium to push them along."

At the end of the semester, the two control groups showed no epistemologic development, but the experimental group showed a statistically significant improvement.

Why might that be? Keesing proposed that understanding of the importance of evidence influences how people acquire general knowledge and that teaching science might be a way to get people to understand the nature of evidence better. "One could say that a core aspect of science is the collection and interpretation of evidence. We have a basic process of acquiring scientific knowledge that rests on the quality of evidence. In a large sense, the scientific method is basically a process of ensuring quality control in the evidence we collect. We use controls, replication, and experimental design to ensure the quality of our evidence. Scientific knowledge is also probabilistic. Finally, some would argue that there are societal and cultural influences on the questions that we ask. For example, it is likely that the recent interest in biocomplexity arose not by chance but because of societal recognition for how it can impact humans in many ways."

One other way to use science and its emphasis on evidence to influence epistemologic development would be to teach modeling, Keesing suggested. "Modeling, for example, the nitrogen cycle involves both subjective and objective knowledge. The art of modeling involves the balance of subjective and objective approaches, even though we often teach modeling as if models were purely objective. Students at the right level could be greatly affected by learning about modeling, and this could greatly improve their epistemologic development as well."

Improving epistemologic development by engaging students in scientific research is one way to approach integrating education and research, but it epitomizes a common theme that carried through the entire workshop. Scientists should not be wary of educational projects or experiments. If they approach them as they would any research project, they can rely on all that they have learned about the scientific method to guide them from project design to evaluation.

- Communicating difficult scientific concepts at different grade levels.
- Simplifying concepts without making them simplistic.
- Time limitations.
- Convincing administrators and peers of the value of participating in such a program.

Case Study 4
Monica Elser, Arizona State University—Central Arizona-Phoenix Long-Term Ecological Research

The Central Arizona-Phoenix Long-Term Ecological Research (CAP LTER) (*http://caplter.asu.edu/*) project is one of 24 long-term sites funded by the National Science Foundation. LTER sites have tended to focus on pristine locations well removed from the myriad effects of human modification and dominance of ecosystems. The CAP LTER site constitutes a unique addition to the LTER research by focusing on an arid-land ecosystem and is one of only two sites that specifically study the ecology of urban systems. Biological, physical, and social scientists from Arizona State University and a wide array of local partners are working together to study the structure and function of the urban ecosystem, assess the effects of urban development on the Sonoran Desert, and define the impact of ecological conditions on urban development.

CAP LTER's investigations into the relationship between land-use decisions and ecological consequences in the rapidly growing urban environment of Phoenix are of broad relevance for urban planning. The project also has an explicit commitment to engage the broader community in this research effort, both in K-16 education and in the public understanding of science.

CAP LTER researchers from Arizona State University work with K-12 educators throughout Phoenix and central Arizona studying urban ecology, so every schoolyard is a study site. The investigations were chosen because of the interest they held for researchers, students, and teachers; they were easy to do and low-tech; they could meet standards for "doing science"; and they could be done in parallel by the students and research faculty.

Students and teachers across the Phoenix metropolitan area collect data on insects, birds, and plants, and they test hypotheses about the impact of urbanization on their local ecosystem. The goal of this approach is to encourage scientific literacy and to contribute to the long-term monitoring of the desert city. Since 1998, the Ecology Explorers (the student and teacher component of CAP LTER) has come to involve 77 teachers in 59 schools in grades 4-10. University faculty and postdoctoral scientists work with education staff and students in the program. CAP LTER includes the following education goals:

- To develop modules based on experiments being carried out by project scientists

- To aim modules at core concepts and inquiry skills already being taught in schools
- To help teachers and students collect real data that would be integrated into the CAP LTER database, thereby vastly expanding coverage of the project
- To work with teachers through workshops and visits to classrooms

The project will be featured in *Chain Reaction* (*http://chainreaction.asu.edu/*), a magazine highlighting the combined efforts of students and scientists.

Current teacher participants in Ecology Explorers go through initial interviewing, a 2-day summer workshop with scientists and previous teacher participants, workshops during the school year based on teacher feedback (topics include mapping, data analysis, and insects in the classroom), preservice and inservice workshops looking for curricula, and a 4-week summer internship working alongside researchers. Throughout the year, teachers and researchers are connected via a community Web site where each protocol or project is clearly explained and teachers may enter data collected by their students that researchers may then use in their work.

According to Elser, "reaction of teachers to the program has been generally positive. They like bringing the concepts of inquiry and best practices into the classroom, and they feel that students benefit from interaction with authentic investigators, learning how to do research and gaining hands-on experience. Students also appreciate recognizing their local environments as ecological systems rather than thinking of ecology as belonging solely to far-off rain forests. There have been inconsistencies in teachers entering collected data into the community Web site, but researchers have been able to use some of the data collected." (See Appendix D for an evaluation of this project.)

Potential benefits for teachers:

- Students may develop a passion for the subject based on the science experience.
- Experiencing the excitement of scientific discovery.
- Becoming more comfortable with science and more willing to take risks.

Potential challenges for teachers:

- Finding scientists willing to listen and learn from the teachers.
- Developing trust with scientists rather than being intimidated.
- Having little time for new curricula (and being even more strapped for resources and time than scientists).
- Persuading school administrators to support the program.

John Farrington, of the Woods Hole Oceanographic Institution (WHOI), encouraged attendees to engage researchers at all levels in educational activities: "Involve graduate students and postdoctoral researchers, and even take advantage of the experience of an institution's alumni who are in K-12 education or informal education."

WHOI is a private, independent, not-for profit corporation dedicated to research and higher education at the frontiers of ocean science. "Since the founding of the institute," Farrington explained, "a philosophy of research being integrated with education in a one-to-one or small-group mode has governed its academic programs and education efforts." The institute is involved in education activities involving partnerships between principal investigators and K-12 teachers and multimedia materials for K-12 education, in addition to activities for undergraduate and general public audiences.

A standard of excellence is demanded of education projects at WHOI, just as is required of research endeavors. As Farrington noted, "not all the world's best scholars are necessarily the world's best teachers and mentors." Staff scientists volunteer for education projects and are compensated for their participation. Projects include local, statewide, and national or international outreach. On a local level, principal investigators work with educators in a science and technology education partnership geared to bringing research and researchers into nearby classrooms. They also participate in local science fairs. At the state level, the institute sponsors summer fellowships for teachers, hosts a regional competition for the National Ocean Sciences Bowl *(www.nosb.org)*, and conducts the Massachusetts Marine Educators annual meeting (*http://www.marine-ed.org/*).

The institute created books and Web-based tools to integrate its research into education activities. The books - which are not textbooks, but classroom-ready material about exciting scientific breakthroughs in ocean research—are geared to students in grades 4-6. WHOI researchers have also been involved in the development of "living textbooks," or modules for use in science education, and a large interactive Web site called "Dive

Case Study 5
Elizabeth Carvellas, Essex, Vermont —Teachers Experiencing the Arctic and Antarctic (TEAA)

Through this program, elementary- and secondary-school teachers participate in field research with National Science Foundation-funded scientists, experience total immersion in research projects, and take what they have learned back to share with students and other teachers. The goal of the program is to help teachers to understand the scientific process, what it means to do science, and that science is ever-changing and often tedious and repetitive. Teachers are involved in planning the project and sit on the advisory board with scientists, helping to shape the program.

In summer 2002, Carvellas went to sea aboard the U.S. Coast Guard cutter *Healy* for a 40-day cruise departing from Nome, Alaska. The cruise was part of a 10-year project, the Shell Station Initiative, looking at carbon cycling in the Arctic Ocean. During the cruise, she was responsible for being part of the research team and for posting daily journal entries and photographs on a Web site to be shared with students (*http://tea.rice.edu/tea_carvellas frontpage.html*). As she explained, she worked with one of the principal investigators on board to "translate the science done on the cruise for the general public to understand."

and Discover" (*www.divediscover.whoi.edu*), which was developed with the idea of reaching out to groups that had little exposure to the ocean. The institute formed a partnership with the Center of Science and Industry in Ohio to build the Web site, where students and educators, or the public at large, can learn about the science being conducted and about the day-to-day life of the crew on a sea-faring research vessel.

Betty Carvellas, of Essex High School in Essex Junction, Vermont (see Case Study 5) gave the audience advice on creating partnerships with K-12 teachers, underscoring the use of existing research. As she put it, "it is important not only to know content, but to know how to translate it into information for kids. An extensive research base for doing this already exists." She also recommended that scientists familiarize themselves with teaching standards and benchmarks. Two important documents for working within curriculum standards are *Benchmarks for Science Literacy* (*http://www.project2061.org/tools/bsl/default.htm*) and *Atlas for Science Literacy*

The application process to become part of TEAA is extensive and requires a commitment from the school system to show that the teacher's school district is supportive of the project. After selection, there is a 1-week orientation that includes survival techniques, ways to translate science for a broad audience, and how to use the experience for professional development for other teachers. Teachers and principal investigators who participate in the project then meet.

After the research experience, which is only a small part of the entire project, there is time for participating teachers to return home and reflect on what was learned, something teachers rarely get a chance to do. Carvellas is responsible for developing two classroom activities that will be peer-reviewed to make sure that they are inquiry-based activities and that they are based on relevant science-education standards. She is also required to work with at least three teacher colleagues at her school, face-to-face, for 140 hours each, over a 3- to 4-year period.

One important goal of this project is to develop teacher leaders. Experiences like this can happen with a few teachers, and the goal is to spread the wealth of experience so that other teachers will gain from it, even if only vicariously.

Finally, Carvellas is responsible for an annual report after she returns from the field, summarizing her experiences for her peers and students and for the National Science Foundation.

(*http://www.project2061.org/tools/atlas/default.htm*); both are products of the American Association for the Advancement of Science.

Carvellas noted that research scientists working with K-12 teachers could influence their communities. "Our citizenry votes on incredibly important issues that are greatly impacted by science and technology issues. Teachers who are well informed can help to create well-informed students so that these students will bring to their society a fuller understanding of science and technology and how they interact with the world." She also noted the similarity between the vocations of teaching and research: "Scientists and teachers share the passion and joy of learning, and both are passionate about their professions. They also share the contradictory public mistrust and blind faith of the public, who may think poorly of the education system at large or scientists in general while still having great respect for their local schools and individual researchers."

Case Study 6
Museums
Cary Sneider, Boston Museum of Science—
"Nowcasting" Project

The field of weather, weather forecasting, or meteorology is one to which anyone can relate. Most people are curious about the local weather on any given day, and many rely heavily on television meteorologists to give them information. "So," Sneider explains, "along with a group of meteorologists and atmospheric scientists, the museum designed a program called 'nowcasting.' Nowcasting means making a prediction about how the weather will be in a particular location in a few hours, or at most, a day."

Many people will look at the Doppler radar, look at the last few hours of activity in their particular area, see how rain is progressing, and make a prediction as to whether they'll see rain at their own homes. Of course, there are only a limited number of sources of Doppler radar data, and they vary widely at times, making it interesting to contrast different sources but also making it difficult to rely on one source for an accurate prediction of whether it will rain in one specific neighborhood.

Weather is more complicated than Doppler radar can indicate, especially to atmospheric scientists who develop the processes and the instrumentation to make predictions about the weather. "The idea is not to have visitors walk away from an exhibit saying, 'Gee, all I have to do is check the Doppler radar, and that's what these meteorologists get paid for'", said Sneider. There is a component of the project that, in more detail, explains mathematical models and

To facilitate the relationship between researchers and schoolteachers, Carvellas recommended that "scientists work with teachers to see what kinds of information will fit well within the curriculum and not assume that just anything provided to teachers will be useful or possible to integrate into the classroom." Many teachers have had unpleasant experiences with scientists who initially offer help, but do not follow through and work to sustain a long-term partnership. Issues related to partnership formation are discussed in the summary section "Getting Started Forming Collaborations."

the deeper philosophic issues that meteorologists and atmospheric scientists address, such as whether it is even possible to make a precise weather prediction.

The goal of the exhibit is to help people to learn about the nature and process of science through weather. Meteorologists collect data from various sources, draw patterns, form hypotheses, and, as the weather system moves, test their hypotheses. Many also run mathematical models using computers to find out what might happen. Like other scientists, meteorologists will make statistical arguments to form their predictions. This method of doing science is explained in the context of a phenomenon that affects everyone everyday.

There is a room in the Museum of Science that is three stories tall and has two large balls on two columns—a van der Graaf generator. This generator produces sparks that are 20 feet long and is used to demonstrate the production of lightning. With additional funding, there will be a feeling of a whole storm in the room during the presentations. Presentations like this get people's attention and draw them in to specific exhibits around the room that illustrate various aspects of nowcasting.

In addition to the exhibits, there are a number of interlocking programs. There are teacher workshops and a Web site where people can do nowcasting. A number of area schools participate in the WeatherNet project. Students in these schools collect data and share them via the Internet. Some of the students will be in the exhibit areas on the weekends and during the summer to interpret their data to the public. (See Appendix D for an evaluation of this project.)

COMMUNITY OUTREACH—EDUCATION PROJECTS OUTSIDE THE EDUCATIONAL SYSTEM

Cary Sneider, of the Museum of Science in Boston, Massachusetts (see Case Study 6) spoke of the advantages of having scientists interact with the public through informal education venues. The public can benefit from the expertise of the scientists and their knowledge of both scientific history and modern applications. However the scientific information must be presented in an accessible format. "The informal education arena—science centers, zoos, arboreta, and so on—offer a diverse audience of visitors. Many are voters—parents or grandparents bringing children to the museum. Classes of schoolchildren also come through with teachers and chaperones, providing a challenging opportunity to reach a wide variety of people who can take the knowledge they gained from an exhibit into various aspects of society." On a much larger scale than individual principal investigators can approach, public outreach programs such as those outlined by Cary Sneider and Kim Kastens, of Columbia University (see Case Study 7), can provide ideas to scientists for education projects.

WORKING WITH JOURNALISTS AND OTHER GROUPS THAT INFLUENCE THE PUBLIC

Journalists communicate with adults, and adults make decisions. Compared with K-12 or even undergraduate audiences, journalists (or attorneys, physicians, or clergy members) deal in an immediate way with adults who make decisions about how society is run. They reach adults by warning them that a decision has to be made or a vote has to be cast or money has to be spent.

Scientists and journalists share many values. Both are strongly driven by curiosity, but a curiosity that is laced with skepticism and a "show-me" attitude. Kastens believes that both are driven by a sense that searching for the truth is important—that the truth exists and it is imperative to find it and communicate it to people.

HOW TO WORK WITH JOURNALISTS

One possibility is to work with journalists and journalism educators to expand the public's understanding of science. Another strategy is to think about the potential value of a research experience for people who are on a preprofessional track that will not lead them into science.

Researchers could approach the journalism schools at their own universities about developing a course in science writing with a journalism professor or even acting as guest professors in this type of course. The Society of Environmental Journalists and the National Association of Science Writers have panels and lists of experts through whom researchers can gain exposure to journalism professionals who are interested in science. Researchers also could meet with the science or environmental writers of their newspapers and take it upon themselves to help better understand and appreciate the nature of science and the kinds of issues and problems that science can and cannot address.

Case Study 7
Kim Kastens, Columbia University, Lamont-Doherty Earth Observatory Environmental Journalism Program

Kim Kastens oversees a 2-year environmental journalism program at Columbia University. Students who have an undergraduate background in science and a demonstrated writing ability are recruited to the program. Students spend 1 year on a master's-level research project and investigate how science is communicated to the public. In their second year, they complete a journalism master's program so that they graduate with two master's degrees—one in journalism and one in environmental and earth sciences. The goal of the program is to prepare journalists who have both the scientific background and the communications skills to inform the public about insights, discoveries, and the environment in ways that are interesting and accurate.

Journalists sometimes find it strange to undertake a scientific research project, but it is consistent with the scientific community's emphasis on integrating research and education. It also gets future journalists to think about processes of science and how the scientific community works. Through this process, students come to understand better the process of floundering around at the boundary between the known and the unknown. By learning skills and techniques in one particular subdiscipline, they begin to understand that research is both a craft and a process. They experience the thrills and challenges of generating original data and thereby come to appreciate the ambiguities and complexities in a field of study.

Kastens noted that "although it has not been difficult to find researchers willing to mentor these students—researchers do want to work with young minds if the structure is right, considering their own constraints—a challenge has come when researchers try to lure students away from the program and into the laboratory for a PhD track. Researchers must respect the fact that there are other legitimate career goals for which an exposure to science is beneficial—that people don't need to end up as research scientists to make it worth while."

The program works with the National Association of Black Journalists, the Native American Journalists Association, and the National Hispanic Journalists Association to recruit minority-group members into this profession. These associations provide funds for fellowships, allowing minority-group journalists to attend meetings of the Society of Environmental Journalists. That is important because the coverage of science and the environment is often poor in media that are targeted to minority populations. (See Appendix D for an evaluation of this project.)

ASSESSING THE PROGRESS AND EFFICACY OF PROJECTS

Diane Ebert-May, of Michigan State University, spoke to the workshop audience about assessment and evaluation of projects. She began by challenging the audience to think of assessment in terms of what kinds of evidence they would find acceptable for measuring progress and outcomes in the research components of their projects. "Assessment is data collection with a purpose," she said. "In research projects, principal investigators collect data with the purpose of answering a question or hypothesis. In education projects, data are collected to answer questions about student learning and instruction. If education projects are considered in the same way as research projects, assessment must be done at appropriate intervals throughout the project." When making decisions about assessing learning, she explained, one should consider how a similar assessment would be done for scientific work. Ebert-May then turned to what she defined as the parallels of assessment in research and education:

- Observations and questions are asked that are meaningful, interesting, and fundable.
- Questions form the basis of assessment.
- Data collected are aligned with a question about a problem. When researchers use the wrong tool or the wrong process, they end up with meaningless data.
- Instruments and techniques are used that are accepted in the field and that stand up to peer review.
- Results are explained in the context of a question.
- Ideas are peer reviewed for merit, publication, dissemination, and funding.

Assessment of learning poses a challenge, but it is possible within the context of the science disciplines and with knowledge from the social sciences.

Collins spoke about evaluation and assessment in her presentation, "Model for Successful Partnerships with K-12 Educators (Science for Early Adolescence Teachers)" (Science FEAT: *http://www.serve.org/Eisenhower/FEAT.html*).

Science FEAT was a 3-year teacher-enhancement program for middle-school teachers of science based at Florida State University and supported by NSF. Sixty-five middle-school teachers in northern Florida and southern Georgia completed the program. Science FEAT received the 1995 Innovation in Teaching Science Teachers Award from the Association for the Education of Teachers in Science and was recognized by the Florida Postsecondary Education Planning Commission as an exemplary initiative program in mathematics-, science-, and technology-related education.

Collins and her colleague at Science FEAT, Sam Spiegel, carried out a formative assessment of the program with data analysis and teacher interviews. They developed a model to evaluate science-school partnerships that was based on three main considerations:

- *Cognitive aspects of the partnership.* Why is the program worth the teachers' time? What makes this knowledge worth while? How does it align with the purpose of schooling? How does it align with state or national standards?
- *Variable expertise.* When multiple communities come together to talk about improving opportunities for students, they should avoid jargon. One way to get around jargon is to draw out a concept map to identify where there might be gaps in understanding. Concept maps are two-dimensional, hierarchic representations of concepts and of relationships between concepts that model the structure of knowledge possessed by a learner or expert. The theory of learning that underlies concept mapping recognizes that all meaningful learning builds on the learner's existing relevant knowledge and the quality of its organization.[1]
- *How people learn.* The National Academies 2000 report *How People Learn* (*http://www.nap.edu/catalog/9853.html?se_side*) elucidates aspects of learning.

    - o *Students come to experiences with prior knowledge.* Humans are viewed as goal-directed agents who actively seek information. They come to formal education with a range of prior knowledge, skills, beliefs, and concepts that significantly influence what they notice about the environment and how they organize and interpret it. This, in turn, affects their abilities to remember, reason, solve problems, and acquire new knowledge.
    - o *Valuable learning experiences, by definition, are meaningful.* A

[1]Free software that aids in the construction of concept maps is available at *www.cmap.coginst.uwf.edu.* (Source: *Learning and Understanding,* National Research Council, 2002.)

corollary is that hands-on or concrete experiences precede learning in the abstract.

o *Understanding implies a rich and useful network of knowledge.* Facts alone, although necessary, are not sufficient for full understanding of a subject. Students must know the "why" behind the facts to truly understand.

o *Learning communities are venues to try out new ideas.* Although students must have the intellectual, physical, and practical tools to accomplish their assigned tasks before working in a group can be productive, a group is an opportunity to try out ideas. Does my idea help me describe, explain, or predict the phenomenon with which I am dealing?

o *Reflection is necessary for analysis.* If active learning is what we want for students, they must have time to reflect and analyze information that is presented to them.

Evaluation is an important part of any research or educational project. In addition to the work of the students, the program itself should be assessed. Some ways to do this are formative evaluations (evaluating programs while they are forming or happening) for program elements (based on opinions of students and faculty), tracking papers and talks (how many, where, and so on), and gathering statistics on students regarding what they did or did not gain from the program, and whether they reached their own goals. These kinds of evaluation may become more and more important. Research experiences are expensive, so researchers will have to be able to demonstrate the value of specific experiences if they are to continue.

PUTTING IT ALL TOGETHER: AN OVERVIEW OF WHY EDUCATION PROPOSALS ARE UNIQUE

A brief presentation by David Mogk, of Montana State University, titled "What's Different About Education Proposals?" was based on A *Guide for Proposal Writing* prepared by the NSF Directorate for Education and Human Resources (*http://www.nsf.gov/pubs/1998/nsf9891/nsf9891.htm*). Mogk emphasized that any good proposal begins with a clear idea of goals and objectives and a sense of why the proposed project will be a substantial improvement over current practice. "Proposals should be innovative within their contexts, describe resources that will be needed, refer to prior work, and, where possible, present evidence of preliminary work by the principal investigators. Education proposals also should address goals that are specific to education and human-resource development. Target audiences need to be clearly identified, and collaborations and coalitions necessary to complete the project successfully (e.g., between scientists, science educators, and developers of instructional materials) should be described in detail. Prospective applicants should seek advice from the program officer or access the abstracts of recently funded projects and contact their principal investigators."

Review of proposals at NSF are considered according to two criteria: intellectual merit and broader impacts. Questions about the intellectual merit of an education proposal might include these:

- Does the project have potential for improving student learning of important principles of science, mathematics, engineering, or technology?"
- Is the project informed by research in teaching and learning, current pedagogical issues, what others have done, and relevant literature?
- Does the project design consider the background, preparation, and experience of the target audience?
- Does the project have the potential to provide fundamental improvements in teaching and learning through effective uses of technology?
- Is the project led by and supported by the involvement of capable faculty (and where appropriate, practicing scientists, mathematicians, engineers, technicians, teachers, and student assistants), who have recent and relevant experience in education, in research, or in the workplace?
- Is the project supported by adequate facilities and resources, and by an institutional and departmental commitment?

More information on implementation of the NSF broader-impacts review criterion can be found at *http://www.nsf.gov/od/opp/opp_advisory/oaccrit2.htm.* Mogk offered the following examples of how this criterion could be applied to education proposals (NSF 98-91):

- To what extent will the results of the project contribute to the knowledge base of activities that enhance student learning?
- Are the proposed course, curriculum, faculty or teacher professional development, experiential learning, or laboratory activities integrated into the institution's academic program?

- Are the results of the project likely to be useful at similar institutions?
- What is the potential for the project to produce widely used products?
- Does the project address the current and future needs of industry for technicians?
- Will the project result in solid content and pedagogical preparation of faculty and teachers?
- Does the project effectively address one or more of the following objectives:

  - o ensure the highest quality education for those students planning to pursue STEM [science, technology, engineering, and mathematics] careers?
  - o increase the participation of women, underrepresented minorities, and persons with disabilities?
  - o provide a foundation for scientific, technological, and workplace literacy?

- Are plans for evaluation of the project appropriate and adequate for the project's size and scope?

With respect to the final point on evaluation, Mogk noted that, although evaluation and dissemination plans are essential for education proposals, program officers report that they are often the weakest parts of education proposals. Evaluation plans will provide information as the project is developing and determine whether the overall project has met the investigator's scientific and pedagogic expectations. Dissemination is at the core of all education projects, and it is essential that information about the success and content of a project be communicated to other scientists and educators.

Researchers and educators alike should anticipate and plan for changes in current educational venues. As Farrington noted, "future learning environments are unknown, but we must anticipate the need for multimedia tools and new formats for the next-generation equivalent of the great textbooks." John Jungck added "Researchers should look to be capturing revolutions in science education. It has been said that science education in the 21st century will have to be integrative, multivariate, multi-level, and multidimensional."

As biocomplexity researchers or others grapple with the new challenges of incorporating educational components into their research, they can look to the advice of the workshop presenters. Overall, as framed by Levitan, if researchers would consider the development of education projects in the same ways they develop research projects, they could more easily identify and reach their goals.

In a presentation of his summative thoughts on the workshop, John Jungck put forth several questions to consider when striving to integrate research and education, "Has background work been done? Has the education research that is relevant to a project been considered; are there related projects that NSF, NIH (National Institutes of Health) or USDA (U.S. Department of Agriculture) funded? Have the available resources in terms of curricular materials, laboratories, classroom exercises, and software, been tapped? What do the students or audience expect? Many students are adults; they are taxpayers; they are putting a great deal of effort into their education—we don't want to waste their time. Is there enough time in the project's schedule for them to accomplish their goals? The definition of 'colleague' should be expanded to include the students and/or the audience. Researchers should respect the recipients of their knowledge, what these recipients know already, and the diversity of their backgrounds and talents."

Levitan's ideas for collaboration were echoed by many at the workshop, whose suggestions covered a wide array of potential collaborative sources. From the interdisciplinary nature of biocomplexity to the interactions involving scientists with undergraduates, elementary students, K-12 teachers, lawmakers, journalists, or others, workshop presenters continually pointed to the benefits of establishing, fostering, and maintaining relationships with other scientists who are committed to improving education and with those who have specific educational or related expertise.

The workshop planning group aimed to provide attendees and those who read this summary with tools for integrating education into research, and this summary is structured with that goal in mind. As Lou Gross described the intent of the workshop and of this summary, he indicated his thoughts on the role of researchers in the scientific community and society at large: they are uniquely positioned to learn about their world and how it works and to share this knowledge with society for the good of all.

Appendix A

Charge to the Planning Group

A workshop will be held that will assist principal investigators in the NSF's Biocomplexity initiative and other scientists who are required to integrate education with research and to communicate and to educate the public more effectively about the nature and significance of their research. Scientists and educators with expertise in fields related to the environment or biocomplexity who have successfully integrated education or outreach components with their research will be invited to give formal presentations about those experiences. They will be asked to describe how they were successful in integrating educational improvement or outreach with their research, and to discuss various approaches to integrating education and research. They will comment on successful ways that principal investigators can design projects where the integration of education and research is an expected outcome of scientific work. The workshop will also include participants in the NSF Biocomplexity grant competition, which requires grantees to incorporate education components into their research. The grantees will learn from the other invited participants and help shape the discussion topics and focus of the workshop. A workshop summary will be prepared describing the discussions that take place at the meeting. These descriptions of projects will serve as examples for investigators in the NSF Biocomplexity Program and many other researchers who must design and implement educational components of a research project.

Appendix B
Biographical Information on Planning Group Members and Workshop Speakers

WORKSHOP PLANNING GROUP

Chair **Louis J. Gross** is professor of ecology and evolutionary biology and mathematics and director of the Institute for Environmental Modeling at the University of Tennessee, Knoxville. His research is in computational ecology. He has led the development of a framework to model the biotic impacts of alternative water planning for the Everglades of Florida and has co-directed courses in mathematical ecology and in quantitative skills for biology students. He is the president-elect of the Society for Mathematical Biology and chair of the Theoretical Ecology Section of the Ecological Society of America. He served as a member of the Panel on Mathematics and Computer Science for the recently released National Research Council report *Bio2010: Transforming Undergraduate Education for Future Research Biologists*. He has received several National Science Foundation grants for undergraduate education and has been active in promoting quantitative training for undergraduate life science students. He designed a year-long course for biology majors to take instead of the traditional calculus course; it shows how mathematical and analytic tools may be used to explore biologic phenomena. He received a BS from Drexel University and a PhD in applied mathematics from Cornell University.

Carol Brewer is an associate professor in the Division of Biological Sciences, an adjunct associate professor in the Department of Curriculum and Instruction, and director of undergraduate studies in biology at the

University of Montana. Her research interests include plant physiologic ecology and functional plant morphology, conservation biology of austral ecosystems, and ecology education. She serves on the Governing Board and is vice president for education of the Ecological Society of America, and she is on the *American Biology Teacher* Journal Advisory Committee. She received a Fulbright Senior Research Award to Argentina. She has been awarded numerous grants by the National Science Foundation and directs the Howard Hughes Medical Institute program at the University of Montana. Dr. Brewer is a member of the National Research Council Committee on Science Education, K-12. She received a PhD in botany from the University of Wyoming.

Diane Ebert-May is a professor in the Department of Plant Biology and director of Assessment in Science Education in the College of Natural Science at Michigan State University. She has served on the Education and Human Resources Committee for the Ecological Society of America, as a member of the National Research Council Committee on Evaluating Undergraduate Teaching, as a member of the Board of Directors, National Association of Research in Science Teaching, and is a fellow of the American Association for the Advancement of Science. Her research group is developing and testing a Web-based concept-mapping tool that enables students in large (and small) science courses to visualize their thinking online as well as to receive immediate feedback. In addition, she is funded by the National Science Foundation to develop a national dissemination network for science-faculty professional development in teaching through biologic field stations and marine laboratories (FIRST II, Faculty Institutes for Reforming Science Teaching). Her research continues on Niwot Ridge, Colorado, where she has conducted long-term research on alpine tundra plant communities since 1971. She received her BS in botany from the University of Wisconsin, Madison, and her MA and PhD in environmental, population, and organismal biology from the University of Colorado, Boulder.

David Mogk is a professor of geology at Montana State University (MSU), Bozeman, Montana. He is currently the collections coordinator for the Digital Library for Earth System Education, a facility that is aggregating and distributing high-quality educational resources to enhance learning about the earth. He served on the interim Coordinating Committee of the National Science, Mathematics, Engineering and Technology Education Digital Library and was coeditor of *Pathways to Progress: Vision and Plans for Developing the NSDL.* He has served as program director in the

Division of Undergraduate Education at the National Science Foundation and is past chair of the Education Committee and Education Division of the Geological Society of America. At MSU, he has been the recipient of the Burlington Northern Award for Excellence in Teaching and the College of Letters and Sciences Distinguished Teaching Award. He is also the recipient of the American Geophysical Union Excellence in Geophysical Education Award (2000). His research interests include the evolution of ancient (over 2.5-billion-year-old) continental crust and attendant petrologic processes and spectroscopy of mineral surfaces and the search for life in extreme environments (from Yellowstone hot springs to Lake Vostok ice core); he is co-principal investigator in the Image and Chemical Analysis Laboratory at MSU. He received a BS from the University of Michigan and an MS and a PhD from the University of Washington.

Joan B. Rose is an international expert in water-pollution microbiology and the Homer Nowlin Chair of Water in Agricultural and Natural Resources Systems at Michigan State University. She was previously at the College of Marine Sciences of the University of South Florida. At the National Research Council, she is the vice chair of the Water Science and Technology Board, a member of the Board on Life Sciences, a member of the Committee on Climate, Ecosystems, Infectious Diseases, and Human Health, and a member of the Committee on Indicators for Waterborne Pathogens. Previous National Research Council service includes membership on the Committee on Wastewater Management for Coastal Urban Areas, the Committee on Drinking Water Contaminants, and the Committee on the Evaluation of the Viability of Augmenting Potable Water Supplies with Reclaimed Water. She is author or coauthor of more than 140 manuscripts in environmental microbiology and recently published a book on risk assessment of microorganisms. Dr. Rose was named one of the 21 most influential people in water in the 21st century by *Water Technology* in 2000 and was awarded the 2001 Clarke Water Prize. She received a BS in microbiology from the University of Arizona, an MS in microbiology from the University of Wyoming, and a PhD in microbiology from the University of Arizona.

WORKSHOP SPEAKERS

Elizabeth Carvellas is department co-chair and teacher of biology at Essex High School in Essex Junction, Vermont. Her professional interests include interdisciplinary learning, the new National Science Education

Standards, and professional development of teachers. She has led several field studies in biology and art in Andros Island, the Bahamas, and Belize. She designed a course that integrates marine biology, botany, art, photography, and journal writing during eight evening sessions; a pool session to practice snorkeling; and a culminating eight-day field study on Andros Island. Students stay at the Forfar Field Station, run by International Field Studies of Columbus, Ohio. While on the island, each student completes a series of art and biology projects related to the unique aspects of the coral-reef ecosystem and the botany of the region. On returning, students share their work with parents and community members at an evening presentation.

Angelo Collins is executive director of the Knowles Science Teaching Foundation. The mission of the foundation is to enhance the quantity of high-quality high-school science teaching. She began her career as a high-school science teacher and received the National Association of Biology Teachers Outstanding Teacher Award. She has had the opportunity to serve as the director of the Teacher Assessment Project at Stanford University, which provided research to inform the National Board for Professional Teaching Standards. She was the director of the project that produced the National Science Education Standards. She also was the principal investigator for ScienceFEAT (Science for Early Adolescence Teachers), an award-winning program to enhance the science knowledge and pedagogic skills of middle-grades science teachers. Most recently, she has worked with the Interstate New Teacher Assessment and Support Consortium on developing standards and performance-based assessments for beginning science teachers. Her research interests lie at the intersection of science teaching, alternative assessment, and policy. She received her PhD from the University of Wisconsin.

Monica Elser is education liaison for the Center for Environmental Studies at Arizona State University. She developed the Ecology Explorer Web site for the Central Arizona-Phoenix Long Term Ecological Research projects work with K-12 students. She has organized and developed pedagogy seminars for graduate/K-12 fellows and internships and workshops for teachers. She has helped to develop a program to retain minority-group students in the biologic sciences at the University of California, Davis. She has done poster and workshop presentations at various professional meetings, including the Ecological Society of America, the National Science Teacher Association, and the Arizona Association for Environmental Education. She received her BS from the University of Notre Dame, her MS in ecology from the University of Tennessee, Knoxville, and her MEd in curriculum and instruction from Arizona State University

John W. Farrington is associate director for education and dean of Woods Hole Oceanographic Institution (WHOI). He has primary responsibility for all the institution's education programs, especially the joint program with the Massachusetts Institute of Technology in oceanography and applied ocean sciences and engineering. He has oversight responsibility for WHOI participation in the Marine Biological Laboratory-WHOI Library in Woods Hole. His scholarly interests include marine organic geochemistry, biogeochemistry of organic pollutants, biochemistry of marine organisms, environmental quality, and education. He is a trustee of the Bermuda Biological Station for Research and a member of the Board of Trustees of the New Bedford Oceanarium. He has served on committees and panels for international, national, and local organizations including the United Nations Educational Scientific and Cultural Organization-Intergovernmental Oceanographic Commission, the National Research Council, the National Science Foundation, the Office of Naval Research, the National Oceanic and Atmospheric Administration, the Department of Energy, and the Lloyd Center for Environmental Studies. He has participated in four major field programs and eighteen oceanographic cruises, eight as chief scientist. He has been honored by the Massachusetts Marine Educators Association, the University of Rhode Island Alumni Association, the U.S. Geological Survey, and the New England Aquarium. He received a BS and an MS in chemistry from Southeastern Massachusetts University (now University of Massachusetts-Dartmouth) and a PhD in oceanography from the University of Rhode Island.

John Jungck is Mead Chair of the Sciences and professor of biology at Beloit College. He is a fellow of the American Association for the Advancement of Science. Professor Jungck is principal investigator and cofounder of the BioQUEST Curriculum Consortium. Over the last 16 years, he and his colleagues at other institutions have been leading the effort to build the BioQUEST Library, a collection of computer-based tools, simulations, databases, and textual materials that support collaborative, open-ended investigations in biology. The modules are developed on campuses around the country; each simulates or models a different biologic system and allows students to analyze massive amounts of data and visualize the relationships among variables. Each module must involve students actively in learning, go through an intensive peer-review process, and be proved effective in the classroom. His research is in mathematical molecular evolution and computational biology (bioinformatics) and their application to teaching and learning biology.

Kim Kastens is an adjunct professor and codirector of the Earth and Environmental Science Journalism Program at Lamont-Doherty Earth Observatory of Columbia University. As an educator, she is interested primarily in science education for nonscientists. She co-founded the Earth and Environmental Science Journalism program, and she has written educational software to help precollege students learn to read maps and to interpret data from environmental sensors.

Felicia Keesing is assistant professor of biology at Bard College. A community ecologist, she studies the consequences of interactions among species, including how savanna communities in Kenya respond to the removal of large herbivores, such as elephants and zebras. In the United States, she studies how interactions among vertebrate species and their habitats influence Lyme disease risk for humans. She also conducts educational research on how students learn about the nature of knowledge. Her work has been published in a variety of journals, including *Ecology, Conservation Biology, BioScience, Vector-Borne and Zoonotic Diseases,* and *Trends in Ecology and Evolution.* In 2000, she was awarded a Presidential Early Career Award for Scientists and Engineers (PECASE). She received her PhD in 1997 from the University of California, Berkeley.

Herbert Levitan is a section head and program director for the Course, Curriculum and Laboratory Improvement Program and the Director's Award for Distinguished Teaching Scholars at the National Science Foundation. He was a faculty member in the Zoology Department of the University of Maryland, College Park, for more than 20 years and was the senior staff associate at the National Institute of Child Health and Human Development. He has taught graduate and undergraduate courses in neurophysiology, electrophysiology, pharmacology, and cell biology. He was a Fulbright fellow in Yugoslavia. He received his PhD in electrical engineering from Cornell University and did postdoctoral research in neurobiology at the Brain Research Institute of the University of California, Los Angeles, the Centre d'Etude de Physiologie Nerveuse in Paris, France, and the National Institute of Mental Health.

Cathryn A. Manduca is director of the Science Education Resource Center at Carleton College. The center is engaged in several projects that support effective science education nationwide, including development of an on-line community center for the Digital Library for Earth System Education, professional development workshops and on-line resources for geoscience faculty, and an interdisciplinary effort by the National STEM Education Digital Library to understand how faculty engage students with data in their courses. Until June 2001, she was coordinator of the Keck Geology Consortium undergraduate research program, which sponsors up to eight collaborative research projects each year involving students around the country. She serves on the American Geophysical Union Committee for Education and Human Resources and as second vice president of the National Association of Geoscience Teachers. She is coauthor of three reports aimed at mobilizing in the geoscience and digital-library communities: *Shaping the Future of Undergraduate Earth Science Education, The Digital Library for Earth System Education—A Community Plan*, and *Pathways to Progress—Vision and Plans for the National STEM Digital Library.*

M. Patricia Morse is a marine biologist and science educator at the University of Washington (UW). For 34 years, she was professor of biology at Northeastern University. The last 4 of those years were spent as a program director at the National Science Foundation (NSF) in the Division of Elementary, Secondary, and Informal Education as a specialist in biology and environmental science in instructional-materials development. Her work in functional morphology involves microscopic analysis (transmission and scanning electron and confocal microscopy) of the bivalve heart-kidney system and molluscan meiofaunal ecology and systematics studies. She serves as project director for the Independent College Office on an NSF K-12 partnership project and chairs the National Research Council Committee on *Attracting Science and Mathematics Ph.D.s to K-12 Education.* She also serves on the advisory group for the UW Sustaining Seattle Teachers Initiative. Dr. Morse is a past president of Sigma Xi, the Scientific Research Society, and of the American Society of Zoologists (now the Society for Integrative and Comparative Biology) and is a fellow of the American Association for the Advancement of Science. She is a member of the Board of Trustees at Bates College, serves on the editorial boards of *Acta Zoologica* and *American Zoologist*, is vice-chair of the International Union of Biological Sciences Commission for Biological Education, and chairs the Education Committee of the American Institute of Biological Sciences. Dr. Morse received a BS from Bates College and an MS and a PhD from the University of New Hampshire.

Susan Singer is a professor of biology and Humphrey Doerman Professor of Liberal Learning and the director of Carleton College's Center for Learning and Teaching. She has taught introductory biology, plant biology, plant development, and developmental genetics for the last 15 years. Her research focuses on the development and evolution of flowering in plants. She has written numerous scientific publications on plant development, edited a plant-development laboratory manual, and written for college textbooks. She is past chair of the American Society of Plant Biologists Education Committee and a current member of the Education Committee of the Society for Developmental Biology. As a program officer in developmental mechanisms in the Biology Directorate of the National Science Foundation, she was involved in the development of a new funding initiative in the evolution of development and served as the directorate representative to the National STEM Digital Library Initiative. She received a BS and a PhD from Rensselaer Polytechnic Institute.

Cary Sneider is vice president for programs at the Museum of Science in Boston. Before assuming that position, he was the director of astronomy and physics education at the Lawrence Hall of Science, directing state and federal grants, developing new instructional materials, and designing and presenting a wide variety of professional-development experiences for teachers. He has conducted research on how to help students to unravel their misconceptions in science and explored new ways to link science centers and schools to promote student inquiry. He served on the National Research Council's Working Group on Science Content Standards for the National Science Education Standards and in 1997 was awarded the National Science Teachers Association's Citation for Distinguished Informal Science Education. He has been a member of the Creation of Study Environments (COSE) K-12 since 1999.

Benjamin van der Pluijm is professor of geological sciences and director of the interdisciplinary Global Change Program at the University of Michigan. His research interests, structure and tectonics, focus on the deformation of earth materials on all scales, in which he has published over 100 refereed articles. He has also published a textbook and edited several volumes in the field. He is editor of *GEOLOGY*, the leading journal for innovative and provocative contributions in the earth sciences, and serves on several editorial boards. In recent years, his teaching has concentrated on the integration of natural science and social science principles for incoming undergraduates using global environmental change as the central issue. The classes also make extensive use of evaluation instruments and student feedback mechanisms in support of effective learning.

Appendix C

Workshop Information

Agenda for Integrating Education in BioComplexity Research
April 14-16, 2002
National Academy of Sciences
2101 Constitution Ave, NW
Washington, DC 20418

April 14

6:30 Dinner for committee and speakers

8:00 Dessert reception and poster session in the Great Hall

April 15

8:15 Welcome from committee chair
Lou Gross

8:30 Introduction of BioComplexity in the Environment-Education Component
Herbert Levitan of NSF

9:00 Goals for the workshop and uses of the workshop summary
Lou Gross

9:30 Three case study presentations (each followed by small group discussions)
Ben van der Pluijm—undergraduate education
Monica Elser—K-12 education and long term ecological research (LTERs)
Cary Sneider—museums

12:00 Lunch

1:00 Keynote talk
Patricia Morse

2:00 Creating partnerships with K-12 teachers
Elizabeth Carvellas
Angelo Collins
Discussion led by **Carol Brewer**

3:30 Integrating research and education
Felicia Keesing

4:30 Break-out Discussions I
- Leading a Workshop
- Undergraduate Courses and Research
- Forming Partnerships with K-12 Teachers
- Assessment and Collaboration with Education School Colleagues

5:30 Wrap-up comments
Lou Gross

5:30 Dinner

7:00 Break-out Discussions II
- Funding Opportunities for Combining Research and Education
- Integrating Research and Teaching—How to Find Time
- Proposal Writing Tips and Setting Up REU Sites

April 16

9:00 Three case study presentations (each followed by small group discussions)
John Farrington—Woods Hole
Cathy Manduca—sharing information between colleges
Kim Kastens—public understanding of science

12:00 Lunch

1:00 Issues to consider in writing future research proposals with education components.
Discussion about how the projects presented in case studies have enhanced education and outreach
Diane Ebert-May and David Mogk
-Methods for evaluating and assessing success
-Methods for dissemination

2:30 Wrap-up panel with audience participation
Susan Singer, John Jungck, Patricia Morse

3:30 Adjourn

POSTERS PRESENTED AT THE WORKSHOP

Adami, Christoph and Nanlohy, Kaben. California Institute of Technology.
BIOCOMPLEXITY: Bacterial and Computational Experiments to Identify General Principles That Govern the Evolution of Complexity.

Alberti, Marina and Marzluff, John. University of Washington.
Modeling the Interactions Between Urban Development, Land Cover Change, and Bird Diversity.

Bain, Mark. Cornell University.
Physical, Biological, and Human Interactions Shaping the Ecosystems of Freshwater Bays and Lagoons.

Berkman, Paul. Oklahoma State University.
Victoria Land, Antarctica, Coastal Biome—Marine-Terrestrial Interaction Across a High Latitudinal Environmental Gradient.

Boone, Randall and Hobbs, Tom. Colorado State University.
Biocomplexity, Spatial Scale and Fragmentation: Implications for Arid and Semi-arid Ecosystems.

Brumbaugh, Dan. American Museum of Natural History, Center for Biodiversity and Conservation.
Coupled Natural and Human Dynamics in Coral Reef Ecosystems: The Effect of Marine Reserve Network Design and Implementation.

Bryant, Tracey. University of Delaware.
Meta-genome analysis of extreme microbial symbiosis.

Dangelmayr, Gerhard. Colorado State University.
Biocomplexity in African Savannas.

Davis, Elaine and Kolm, Kenneth. Crow Canyon Archaeological Center and Colorado School of Mines.
Coupled Human/Ecosystems over Long Periods: Mesa Verde Region Prehispanic Ecodynamics.

Glazier, James. University of Notre Dame.
Multiscale Simulation of Avian Limb Development.

Gorrell, Thomas. Pace University.
Development of a Biocomplexity Research Program for the Analysis of Ecosystem Structure and Dynamics in Urban Salt Marshes.

Lansing, Stephen and Watkins, Joseph. University of Arizona.
Emergence of Cooperation from Human-Environmental Interactions.

Mazurek, Monica. Rutgers University.
Biocomplexity: The Roles of Resources, Competition, and Predation in Microbial Degradation of Organic Matter.

McGinnis, David. Idaho Sate University.
Modeling Biocomplexity and Socio-economic Decision-making Under Uncertainty in the Greater Yellowstone Ecosystem: A Proposal to Develop an Interdisciplinary Team.

Newmark, William. University of Utah, Utah Museum of Natural History.
Large Mammal Movement Through Complex Landscapes in East Africa.

Pijanowski, Bryan. Michigan State University.
Climate and Land Use Change Processes in East Africa.

Raubeson, Linda. Central Washington University.
Comparative Chloroplast Genomics.

Schofield, Oscar. Rutgers University.
The Evolution and Radiation of Eucaryotic Phytoplankton Taxa.

Swaney, Bill. Salish Kootenai College.
Biocomplexity—Dynamic Controls on Emergent Properties of River Flood Plains.

Weiler, Susan. Whitman College.
Biocomplexity at the Land-Water Interface: Enhancing Interdisciplinary Understanding and Networking Among Recent Graduates.

Greenler, Robin. Beloit College.
BioQuest Curriculum Consortium.

WORKSHOP PARTICIPANTS

Name	**Institution**
Abrajano, Teofilo A.	Rensselaer Polytech Institute
Adami, Christoph	California Institute of Technology
Alberti, Marina	University of Washington
Avila, Bridget	National Research Council
Bain, Mark	Cornell University
Baker, Larry	University of Minnesota
Berkman, Paul	Ohio State University
Blackmore, Denis	Foundation at NJIT
Blockstein, David	National Council for Science and the Environment
Boone, Randall	Colorado State University
Brenner, Kerry	National Research Council
Brewer, Carol	University of Montana
Brumbaugh, Dan	American Museum of Natural History
Bryant, Tracey	University of Delaware

Campbell, David	National Science Foundation
Carter, Celeste	National Science Foundation
Carvellas, Elizabeth	Essex High School
Catena, Anne	Princeton University
Cavanaugh, Margaret A.	National Science Foundation
Chen, Benito	University of Wyoming
Cherry, Lynne	Princeton University
Collins, Angelo	Knowles Science Teaching Foundation
Cook, Susan	National Science Foundation
Dangelmayr, Gerhard	Colorado State University
Davis, Elaine	Crow Canyon
Dybas, Cheryl	National Science Foundation
Ebert-May, Diane	Michigan State University
Elser, Monica	Arizona State University
Farrington, John	Woods Hole Oceanographic Institution
Feng, Zhilan	Purdue University
Firth, Penny	American Association for the Advancement of Science
Glazier, James	University of Notre Dame
Gorrell, Thomas	Pace University
Greenler, Robin	Beloit College
Gross, Louis	The University of Tennessee, Knoxville
Gutmann, Valerie	National Research Council
Hamilton, Bruce	National Science Foundation
Hoagland, Elaine	Council on Undergraduate Research
Hobbs, Tom	Colorado State University
Hofmann, Gretchen	Arizona State University
Hudak, Andrew	University of Idaho
Jarrett, Jeremiah	Central Connecticut State University
Joye, Samantha	University of Georgia
Jungck, John	Beloit College
Kastens, Kim	Columbia University
Keeney, Dennis	Iowa State University
Keesing, Felicia	Bard College
Kolm, Kenneth	Colorado School of Mines
Labov, Jay	National Research Council
Lansing, Stephen	University of Arizona
Levitan, Herb	National Science Foundation
Lundmark, Cathy	American Institute of Biological Sciences

Manduca, Cathryn	Carleton College
Marzluff, John	University of Washington
Mazurek, Monica	Rutgers University
McGinnis, David	Idaho State University
Mead, Pat	National Academy of Engineering
Meyerson, Fred	National Science Foundation
Mogk, David	Montana State University
Morse, Patricia	University of Washington
Nanlohy, Kaben	California Institute of Technology
Newmark, William	University of Utah
Norgaard, Richard	University of California, Berkeley
Nyhus, Philip	Franklin and Marshall College
Pijanowski, Bryan	Michigan State University
Prendeville, Jewel	National Science Foundation
Raubeson, Linda	Central Washington University
Rose, Joan	University of South Florida
Roskoski, Joann	National Science Foundation
Singer, Jill	National Science Foundation
Singer, Susan	Carleton College
Sneider, Cary	Museum of Science in Boston
Suiter, Marilyn	National Science Foundation
Swaney, Bill	University of Montana
Van der Pluijm, Ben	University of Michigan
Verdugo, Pedro	University of Washington
Watkins, Joseph	University of Arizona
Weiler, Susan	Whitman College
White, Michael	Utah State University
Whitmer, Ali	Arizona State University
Woodin, Terry	National Science Foundation
Yuan, Robert	National Research Council
Zachos, Jim	University of California, Santa Cruz

Appendix D Assessment and Evaluation Data on Case Study Projects

This Appendix includes assessment and evaluation data from several of the workshop's case studies. This information is provided to show the variety of approaches used in measuring the effectiveness of a program as judged by its various participants. These data were gathered from presenters and from resources available on the Internet. When known, Web site addresses for the data have been provided.

CASE STUDY 2, BEN VAN DER PLUIJM, GLOBAL CHANGE PROGRAM, UNIVERSITY OF MICHIGAN

Below are data from the end-of-semester survey administered to Global Change I students in fall 1999. [a]

[a]These data were collected by an evaluation team led by Professor Eric Dey (Higher Education, University of Michigan) as part of the School of Education's Undergraduate Curriculum Development Testbed (UCDT). See *http://www.wcer.wisc.edu/nise/cl1/ilt/case/michigan/michigan.htm.*

I. LAB EXPERIENCE

	Strongly Agree	Agree	Neutral	Disagree	Strongly Disagree
1. The lab assignments seem carefully chosen.	12.3%	67.7%	10.8%	4.6%	4.6%
2. The lab assignments are intellectually challenging.	7.7%	72.3%	12.3%	3.1%	4.6%
3. Laboratory assignments make an important contribution to my understanding of the topics discussed in lecture.	7.7%	44.6%	32.3%	7.7%	7.7%
4. *ArcView* has helped me understand Global Change concepts and principles.	13.8%	56.9%	20.0%	4.6%	4.6%
5. I feel confident in my ability to use ArcView to construct models.	24.6%	67.7%	4.6%	3.1%	0.0%
6. ArcView helps me understand the relationships among different variables.	18.5%	63.1%	10.8%	6.2%	1.5%

II. LECTURE EXPERIENCE

	Strongly Agree	Agree	Neutral	Disagree	Strongly Disagree
1. Having several instructors give the lecture contributes to my understanding of the concepts and principles related to Global Change II.	38.5%	46.2%	10.8%	3.1%	1.5%
2. The transition from one instructor to the next interferes with my ability to learn.	6.2%	7.7%	12.3%	66.2%	7.7%
3. I have learned a good deal of factual material in this course.	36.9%	56.9%	6.2%	0.0%	0.0%

	Strongly Agree	Agree	Neutral	Disagree	Strongly Disagree
4. The knowledge I have gained through this course has improved my ability to participate in debates about global change.	30.8%	63.1%	6.2%	0.0%	0.0%
5. This course has encouraged me to think critically about global change.	46.2%	50.8%	3.1%	0.0%	0.0%
6. It is difficult for me to understand how topics covered in the lecture fit together.	3.1%	16.9%	7.7%	60.0%	12.3%

III. WEB EXPERIENCE

	Strongly Agree	Agree	Neutral	Disagree	Strongly Disagree
1. Using the web has made a significant contribution to my learning.	32.3%	50.8%	12.3%	4.6%	0.0%
2. The links from the Global Change website to other internet websites have provided me with helpful information.	15.4%	24.6%	50.8%	6.2%	3.1%
3. I feel confident in my ability to use the web to gather information about global change.	52.3%	41.5%	4.6%	1.5%	0.0%
4. I have used the web skills I have acquired in this course to complete academic work for other classes.	16.9%	43.1%	26.2%	12.3%	1.5%
5. I have utilized the web skills I have developed in this course to investigate areas that interest me.	21.5%	38.5%	29.2%	9.2%	1.5%

IV. PERSONAL GROWTH

	Strongly Agree	Agree	Neutral	Disagree	Strongly Disagree
1. I have deepened my interest in the subject matter of this course.	39.4%	51.5%	6.1%	1.5%	1.5%
2. I am enthusiastic about the course material.	31.8%	50.0%	15.2%	1.5%	1.5%
3. I feel like I make an important contribution to the learning of others in the course.	12.1%	36.4%	40.9%	9.1%	1.5%
4. I have had opportunities to help other students in the course learn about Global Change concepts and principles.	10.6%	42.4%	34.8%	7.6%	4.5%
5. I feel empowered to act on what I have learned.	22.7%	57.6%	16.7%	3.0%	0.0%

CASE STUDY 4 MONICA ELSER, CENTRAL ARIZONA-PHOENIX LONG TERM ECOLOGICAL RESEARCH PROJECT (CAP-LTER), ARIZONA STATE UNIVERSITY

http://caplter.asu.edu/progress.htm
From CAP LTER 2000-2001 Annual Report (the entire report can be found at *http://caplter.asu.edu/progress.htm)*

We reach out to the K-12 community through *Ecology Explorers,* a program that aims to: develop and implement a schoolyard ecology program where students collect data similar to Central Arizona-Phoenix Long Term Ecological Research Project (CAP LTER) data, enter results into our database, share data with other schools, and develop hypotheses and experiments to explain their findings; improve science literacy by exposing students and teachers to real research conducted by university-level scientists; enhance teachers' capabilities to design lessons and activities that use scientific inquiry and encourage interest in science; provide access to and promote the use of CAP LTER materials and information; encourage collaboration between CAP LTER researchers and the K-12 community; provide students an opportunity to share their research with other children, adults, and CAP LTER researchers through poster presentations at SEE ASU and the CAP LTER poster symposium, and through our new Kid's Online Newsletter.

From the initial collaboration sparked with 12 schools in 1998, Ecology Explorers has expanded to include 34 schools, 46 teachers, 14 school districts, and 3 charter schools. Popular summer workshops and internships have engaged numerous teachers in our schoolyard sampling protocols for the vegetation survey, ground arthropod investigation, bird survey, and plant/insect interaction study and biogeochemical cycles.

This year we have developed threenew day-long workshops based on teacher requests. The topics covered in the workshops were: (1) mapping the schoolyard; (2) analyzing data; (3) insects in the classroom. A total of 21 teachers participated in these workshops. The teacher evaluations suggested that these workshops addressed their needs and were beneficial.

This summer's program will include 16 new teachers (2 of whom are from school districts new to our program) and more than 12 ASU personnel. We will be offering two 2-week internships that allow the teachers to participate in a research project and learn how to collect and analyze data. They will be introduced to several hands-on, inquiry-based lessons developed from previous workshops and create new lesson plans that will be added to the Ecology Explorers Web site.

In January 2001, we surveyed our teachers to assess whether our programs are meeting their needs: 79% use our protocols in some way (29% follow the protocols and enter data, 26% conduct the protocols but do not enter data, and 24% pick and choose among parts of the protocols that meet the needs of their class). Eighteen percent were not currently involved but planned to be soon, while 6% had been involved in the past but not currently. Six percent were not currently involved and did not plan to be involved in the future. We also found that 92% of the teachers had worked with the CAP LTER education personnel and that this was an important component of the program. We found that teachers use the Ecology Explorers Web site more than their students. Items that the teachers would like to see included on the Web site were: lesson plans (47%), Web links (47%), extension activities (50%), graphs (53%), easier data entry and retrieval (30%). Teachers consistently reported that the reason they like this program is the integration of real research projects into their curriculum and the support they receive from CAP LTER staff. Participating teachers have applauded Ecology Explorers for the following attributes: "Authentic learning activities for students. Life skills for students. *Outstanding* support from CAP LTER staff. Chance to participate in a long-range project. Good way to integrate skills and curriculum." Based on feedback from teachers, we have developed several new Web features this year (*http://caplter.asu.edu/explorers*): online lesson plans developed by Ecology Explorer teachers, online slide sets, resource lists (Web-based and print),"Meet the Scientist" interviews, and some extension activities for several of the protocols. We have been working with the CAP LTER data personnel to make the data entry and retrieval features easier to use and hope to be able to produce real-time graphs within the next year. We are also working on a flash animation to simulate the ground arthropod protocol.

Through informal discussions with teachers, we know that they have a better understanding of ecological research, students' enthusiasm for projects exceeded expectations, students felt projects were important because of the ASU connection and were willing to put in extra effort to carry out the projects, more parents were involved than anticipated, and workshops/internships were valuable and enhanced their ability to teach science. Teacher's have also reported that students' math abilities improved as a result of participating in Ecology Explorers. Participating in poster presentations enhanced students' communication skills. The program is aligned with the AZ State Education Standards, including science, math, writing, social science, and technology standards.

CASE STUDY 5, BETTY CARVELLAS, ESSEX HIGH SCHOOL, VERMONT

The information below is an excerpt from the TEA Program Evaluation Year Two Report. More information is available at *http://tea.rice.edu.*

Research principal investigators (PIs) saw the experience as improving teachers' scientific research skills, while at the same time helping the researchers and their teams gain a better understanding of K-12 education. One research PI said,

> Our teacher expressed an interest in our research well over a year before joining us in Antarctica. This allowed us to build a strong working relationship well before reaching the field. Before reaching the field and while in the field she continued her strong interest in the underlying experience making her a valuable member of the team. Finally, the improved understanding of the K-

Researcher PIs Overall Assessments (n = 21)

Statement	Strongly Disagree	Disagree	Somewhat Disagree	Somewhat Agree	Agree	Strongly Agree	N/A
1. Having a TEA on my team has been a rewarding experience for me.	—	—	4.8	4.8	19.0	71.4	—
9. Having a TEA teacher on my team helped me and my team gain a better understanding of K-12 education.	—	—	—	23.8	33.3	42.9	—
10. Working with a TEA teacher has provided me a good opportunity to share my research and scientific interests with other teachers and students.	—	—	—	19.0	33.3	47.6	—
25. My TEA teacher gained a better understanding of how scientific research is conducted as a result of being a member of my research team.	—	4.8	—	—	19.0	76.2	—
26. The field research experience increased my TEA teacher's scientific knowledge and skills.	—	—	—	9.5	33.3	57.1	—
30. I would take *another* TEA teacher with me into the field.	—	4.8	—	4.8	28.6	61.9	—
31. I would take the *same* TEA teacher with me into the field again.	4.8	4.8	—	9.5	19.0	61.9	—
32. I would recommend to my colleagues that they take a TEA teacher into the field.	—	—	4.8	9.5	28.6	57.1	—

Teacher's Interaction with PI

Statement	Strongly Disagree	Disagree	Somewhat Disagree	Somewhat Agree	Agree	Strongly Agree	N/A
9. My principal investigator (PI) involved me in a meaningful way in his/her research *before* going into the field.	7.7	7.7	—	23.1	23.1	38.5	—
10. My PI involved me in a meaningful way in his/her research *during* the field research experience.	7.7	—	—	—	38.5	46.2	7.7
11. My PI helped me define a field experience that aligned with my interests.	7.7	7.7	—	7.7	38.5	38.5	—
12. My PI made his/her expectations of me clear before I went into the field.	7.7	—	7.7	15.4	46.2	23.1	—
13. I was able to make my expectations and responsibilities clear to my PI and his/her team before I went into the field.	—	—	7.7	7.7	61.5	23.1	—
14. My PI provided me the time needed during the field experience for me to complete my TEA program responsibilities.	—	—	—	7.7	15.4	76.9	—
15. My PI treated me like a professional.	—	—	—	15.4	15.4	69.2	—
17. I think my PI developed a better understanding of teachers by my involvement in the TEA project.	7.7	—	—	30.8	—	61.5	—
30. My PI has continued to involve me in a meaningful way in his/her research *since* my field research experience.	15.4	23.1	15.4	23.1	15.4	7.7	—

> 12 environment enriched us all, as well as the understanding of what sorts of ideas and activities would translate well to her students.

Another researcher described the experience in these words,

> Overall, the experience was an excellent opportunity for my TEA teacher to learn first hand about Antarctic science and ecology. I gained a tremendous insight, and rewarding experiences, after 2 days of classes teaching junior high students. Every scientist should have this experience.

Based on this survey evidence, several factors in addition to conducting scientific field research itself, contribute to successful field experience for teachers. These include: (1) clear communications of responsibilities and expectations, by both parties, prior to the field work; (2) aligning of field experiences with teachers' interests; (3) involving teachers in meaningful ways in the PIs research projects; and (4) treating teachers like the professionals they are, by both the research PIs and their research teams.

CASE STUDY 6, CARY SNEIDER, MUSEUM OF SCIENCE, BOSTON, MASSACHUSETTS

Predicting the Future: The Science and Technology of Weather Forecasting

NSF Informal Science Education grant to the Museum of Science, Boston. Grant period 8/1/02 to 7/31/05

Despite the important role that weather plays in our lives, misconceptions and ignorance about weather are widespread. Few adults can read a weather map well enough to predict how conditions are likely to change in the next few hours, and most are unaware of typical weather patterns where they live. Yet there is a great deal of interest in the weather, and many people turn on the news just to see the current forecast. In fact, opportunities to learn about the weather through informal means may be one of the best opportunities to teach people about Earth systems. Additionally, meteorologists (atmospheric scientists whom people encounter daily) provide wonderful opportunities to communicate the processes of science, such as data collection and analysis, modeling, and prediction.

This proposal is predicated on the conviction that everyone can make accurate short-term predictions of the weather (called *nowcasting.*) Furthermore, in the process of learning to forecast the weather, learners can deepen their understanding of Earth systems as well as gain insight into the nature of science and technology. To accomplish these goals, experienced Museum of Science personnel will work with meteorologists and other atmospheric scientists to develop a project entitled *Predicting the Future: The Science and Technology of Weather Forecasting,* which will have the following components:

An exhibition on weather will be available to more than 1.2 million people who visit the Museum of Science's exhibit galleries every year. At the exhibit, visitors will learn how to forecast the weather over the next few hours using different levels of technology, including naked eye observations, data from weather maps, and real-time images from space satellites and ground radar stations.

Programs for Students and Teachers will help this important group of visitors make effective use of the exhibition, and extend the field trip by using the interactive website described below. In-depth programs will be provided for teachers and students from more than 100 WeatherNet schools in New England, while other programs will be made available to more than 250,000 students and teachers who visit the Museum every year.

An interactive website will provide guidance in using online weather resources to predict the weather several hours in advance. The website will be accessible to anyone, free of charge, through the Museum's home page, or in the exhibit gallery. While website numbers are difficult to estimate, the audience for this website is at least in the hundreds of thousands.

Television spots will address the broadest audience—mostly adults who tune in the weather broadcast, and who may be open to spending one additional minute to learn something new about the process of weather forecasting. The television spots will be aired on WBZ-TV Channel 4 in the Boston area, shared with CBS affiliates, and provided as part of a larger series of educational programs to The Weather Channel. Viewership is expected to be in the millions.

This project will build on a long-term partnership with WBZ Television and more than 100 local schools in which students and teachers monitor the weather on a continuous basis, providing a dense local network of weather data available to the public via WBZ and Museum of Science websites. Special workshops will be held for WeatherNet teachers, and

WeatherNet students will be invited to serve as volunteer interpreters in the exhibit gallery. WBZ will also create the television spots and provide assistance with other aspects of the overall project. Other partners include TERC in Cambridge, with responsibility for developing the website, AER, Inc. will provide real-time analysis and display of satellite images to simplify interpretation, Blue Hill Meteorological Observatory will serve as one site for teacher education, and Selinda Research Associates, will conduct an independent evaluation of the project.

Evaluation

To ensure that the website, exhibit components, school programs, and TV spots are effectively engineered and coordinated to accomplish the project's goals, a significant portion of the effort will be devoted to evaluation. These evaluation activities will include: (a) front end evaluation to check and refine previous studies concerning people's understanding and misconceptions about weather; (b) formative evaluation to improve the educational effectiveness of the exhibit, programs, and website; and (c) summative evaluation to measure the effectiveness of the overall effort.

Over the years, the Museum of Science has come to appreciate the importance of evaluation for maximizing the potential of creating successful visitor experiences. In "Predicting the Future," evaluation will be planned and implemented by Selinda Research Associates and will be an integral and indispensable component of the overall project. In this project, Selinda Research Associates—in consultation with Museum of Science Staff—will plan and implement three evaluation studies: front-end, formative, and summative.

Front end. This project will require a thorough understanding of the target audiences and their connection to weather. Selinda Research Associates will develop and implement an evaluation study that investigates visitors' preconceptions and understandings of weather. It will investigate the extent to which and the ways in which the potential audience for this project—including users of the exhibition, programs, website, and television spots—think about and understand weather and the process of weather forecasting. It will also assess the ability of different age groups to grasp the requisite concepts and learn forecasting skills.

Beginning with an extensive review of the literature from the fields of the public understanding of science and visitor studies, and building on previous museum evaluation work done on weather-related projects, a preliminary understanding of the target audience will be developed. Building on the knowledge gained from the review of the literature, in-depth interviews will be also be conducted to develop deeper understandings of visitors and weather. Research questions will include: What topics will be most interesting to visitors? How do visitors understand and think about weather and its effect on their lives? What is their understanding of what meteorologists do? How do they interpret weather maps? What questions do they have? What may be effective hooks for them? What misconceptions do they have?

The results of the front-end evaluation study will be summarized and presented to the project team to help inform the planning process.

Formative evaluation will be conducted to identify revisions and improvements to the components of "Predicting the Future." Exhibit prototypes will be tested in the Museum's "Test Tube Gallery." Formative evaluation will also be conducted of the website, TV spots, and the program throughout the development process. Using a rapid-prototyping process, results from the formative evaluation will immediately inform the design/ development decisions. Techniques will include participant and unobtrusive observation, and in-depth interview. Data analysis will use a modified inductive constant comparison approach (Lincoln, Y.S. and E.G. Guba. 1985. *Naturalistic Inquiry.* Beverly Hills, CA: Sage Publication). Questions will include: Can visitors use this component? What seems to work well? What doesn't work as well? How can this component be improved so that more visitors will be able to be more successful? Throughout the formative evaluation process, findings will be quickly communicated to the project team so that changes can be made to the prototype units.

Summative. At the end of the development of the components for this project, it will be important to assess the visitor experience and determine the extent to which the overall effort was successful. Using a combination of tracking and timing, unobtrusive and participant observation, and in-depth exit interviews, the visitor experience will be assessed. Emphasis will be placed on **(a) the outcomes of visitors' experiences** (What did they learn that they didn't know before? Were they able to successfully use what they learned to make weather predictions? Did they develop a greater appreciation for the processes of science? And for the role of mathematics and engineering in weather prediction?) **(b) the ways they engaged** (What did they do? What was the quality and meaningfulness of their social interactions? In what ways were they intellectually engaged?) and **(c) the experience itself** (Did they enjoy themselves? Was their curiosity piqued? Were they appropriately challenged? Did they feel in charge of their learning? Were there opportunities for playfulness?). Data will be gathered and analyzed, and a written evaluation report submitted to the project team and the National Science Foundation. Finally, the Museum of Science has budgeted funds to remediate the exhibit based on the results of the summative evaluation.

Appendix E

Additional Resources

WORKSHOP HANDOUTS ADVICE ON PROPOSAL-WRITING AND PROJECT EVALUATION

Proposal-Writing Aids

A Guide for Proposal Writing, a booklet prepared by staff in DUE (NSF 98-91)
http://www.nsf.gov/pubs/1998/nsf9891/nsf9891.htm

NSF's Step-by-Step Guide for Prospective Principal Investigators, basic tips on exploring funding opportunities at NSF and preparing a proposal
http://www.nsf.gov/home/programs/guide.htm

Frequently Asked Questions: Preparing and Submitting a Proposal to NSF, a list of questions and answers maintained by NSF's Policy Office
http://www.nsf.gov/bfa/cpo/policy/faqs.htm

NSF 00-117: Supplemental Information for Principal Investigators and Applicants to NSF's Course, Curriculum, and Laboratory Improvement Program, a summary of desired objectives for CCLI projects, and approaches to measuring those objectives
http://www.nsf.gov/pubs/2000/nsf00117/nsf00117.htm

Resources for Project Evaluation

NSF 93-152: User-Friendly Handbook for Project Evaluation, a monograph describing the evaluation process, with a focus on the collection and analysis of quantitative data

http://www.ehr.nsf.gov/EHR/RED/EVAL/handbook/handbook.htm

NSF 97-153: User-Friendly Handbook for Mixed Method Evaluations, a monograph "initiated to provide more information on qualitative [evaluation] techniques and ... how they can be combined effectively with quantitative measures"

http://www.ehr.nsf.gov/EHR/REC/pubs/NSF97-153/start.htm

Online Evaluation Resource Library (OERL) for NSF's Directorate for Education and Human Resources, a collection of evaluation plans, instruments, reports, glossaries of evaluation terminology, and best practices, with guidance for adapting and implementing evaluation resources

http://oerl.sri.com/

Field-Tested Learning Assessment Guide (FLAG) for Science, Math, Engineering, and Technology Instructors, a collection of "broadly applicable, self-contained modular classroom assessment techniques and discipline-specific tools for ... instructors interested in new approaches to evaluating student learning, attitudes, and performance."

http://www.wcer.wisc.edu/nise/CL1/flag/

Programs That Support Education at NSF
Cross-Cutting Programs

Career Program
http://www.nsf.gov/home/crssprgm/career/start.htm

NSF Graduate Teaching Fellows in K-12 Education (GK-12)
http://www.nsf.gov/home/crssprgm/gk12/start.htm

IGERT: Integrative Graduate Education and Research Traineeship Program
http://www.nsf.gov/home/crssprgm/igert/start.htm

REU: Research Experiences for Undergraduates
http://www.nsf.gov/home/crssprgm/reu/start.htm

RUI/ROA: Research in Undergraduate Institutions and Research Opportunity Awards
http://www.ehr.nsf.gov/crssprgm/rui/start.shtm

Directorate for Education and Human Resources
http://www.nsf.gov/home/ehr/

Math Science Partnerships (NSF 02-061)
http://www.nsf.gov/pubs/2002/nsf02061/nsf02061.html

Division of Elementary, Secondary and Informal Education (ESIE)
http://www.ehr.nsf.gov/ehr/esie/

Program Solicitation for ESIE
http://www.nsf.gov/cgi-bin/getpub?nsf0160

Centers For Learning and Teaching (CLT) (NSF 02-038)
http://www.ehr.nsf.gov/esie/resources/centers.asp
abstracts and websites of successful proposals

Instructional Materials Development
http://www.nsf.gov/pubs/2002/nsf02067/nsf02067.html

Informal Science Education
http://www.nsf.gov/pubs/1997/nsf9770/isesupl.htm

Teacher Enhancement
http://www.ehr.nsf.gov/rec/publications/eval/tep/tep.htm

Division of Undergraduate Education (DUE)
http://www.ehr.nsf.gov/due/

Advanced Technology Education
http://www.ehr.nsf.gov/due/programs/ate/

Assessment of Student Achievement in Undergraduate Education
http://www.ehr.nsf.gov/due/programs/asa/

Course, Curriculum and Laboratory Improvement
http://www.ehr.nsf.gov/due/programs/ccli/

National STEM Education Digital Library
http://www.ehr.nsf.gov/due/programs/nsdl/

Other Funding Opportunities for Undergraduate STEM Education
http://www.ehr.nsf.gov/due/links/other_programs.asp

Division of Research, Evaluation and Communication (REC)
http://www.ehr.nsf.gov/rec/

Interagency Education Research Initiative (IERI)
http://www.nsf.gov/pubs/2002/nsf02062/nsf02062.html

Research on Learning and Education (ROLE)
http://www.ehr.nsf.gov/rec/

Evaluative Research and Evaluation Capacity Building
http://www.nsf.gov/pubs/2002/nsf0234/nsf0234.html

RESOURCES

David Mogk, of the University of Montana, listed the following as resources within NSF that support educational projects.

Interdisciplinary Programs:
NSF Graduate Teaching Fellowships in K-12 Education (GK-12)

This program supports fellowships and associated training that will enable graduate students and advanced undergraduates in the sciences, mathematics, engineering, and technology to serve as resources in K-12 schools. Academic institutions apply for awards to support fellowship activities, and are responsible for selecting Fellows. The Fellows will serve as resources for teachers in science and mathematics instruction. Expected outcomes include improved communication and teaching skills for the Fellows, enriched learning by K-12 students, professional development opportunities for K-12 teachers, and strengthened partnerships between institutions of higher education and local school districts (from *http://www.ehr.nsf.gov/dge/programs/gk12/*).

IGERT (Integrative Graduate Education and Research Traineeship Program)

The IGERT program has been developed to meet the challenges of educating U.S. Ph.D. scientists, engineers, and educators with the interdisciplinary backgrounds, deep knowledge in chosen disciplines, and technical, professional, and personal skills to become in their own careers the leaders and creative agents for change. The program is intended to catalyze a cultural change in graduate education, for students, faculty, and institutions, by establishing innovative new models for graduate education and training in a fertile environment for collaborative research that transcends traditional disciplinary boundaries. It is also intended to facilitate greater diversity in student participation and preparation, and to contribute to the development of a diverse, globally-engaged science and engineering workforce (from *http://www.nsf.gov/home/crssprgm/igert/intro.htm*).

RUI/ROA: Research in Undergraduate Institutions and Research Opportunity Awards

All NSF directorates participate in the Research in Undergraduate Institutions (RUI) activity, which supports research by faculty members of predominantly undergraduate institutions through the funding of (1) individual and collaborative research projects, (2) the purchase of shared-use research instrumentation, and (3) Research Opportunity Awards for work with NSF-supported investigators at other institutions (from *http://www.ehr.nsf.gov/crssprgm/rui/start.shtm*).

Discipline Specific Programs:

The National Science Foundation funds research and education in science and engineering. It does this through grants, contracts, and cooperative agreements to more than 2,000 colleges, universities, and other research and/or education institutions in all parts of the United States. The Foundation accounts for about 20 percent of federal support to academic institutions for basic research. Each year, NSF receives approximately 30,000 new or renewal support proposals for research, graduate and postdoctoral fellowships, and math/science/engineering education projects; it makes approximately 9,000 new awards. These typically go to universities, colleges, academic consortia, nonprofit institutions, and small businesses.

The agency operates no laboratories itself but does support National Research Centers, certain oceanographic vessels, and Antarctic research stations. The Foundation also supports cooperative research between universities and industry and U.S. participation in international scientific efforts.

Getting Information About NSF Programs

Most NSF funding opportunities are divided into broad program areas:

Biology
Computer and Information Sciences
Crosscutting Programs
Education
Engineering
Geosciences
International
Math, Physical Sciences
Polar Research
Science Statistics
Social, Behavioral Sciences

Information about NSF programs is compiled annually into the Guide to Programs, and updated and supplemented by periodic Program Announcements and Solicitations. These publications can be found through the Online Document System. Lists of current announcements and information can also be found on the NSF web by broad program area. To receive rapid notification of new program information, by email or via a custom web page, you may subscribe to NSF's Custom News Service.

Special Programs

Additional funding opportunities may be found in these special program areas:

For Educators and Faculty
For Students and Post-Doctorates
Multidisciplinary and Joint Agency Programs
Small Business Programs
(from *http://www.nsf.gov/home/programs/start.htm*)

"CREATING RESEARCH OPPORTUNITIES FOR TEACHERS"

BETTY CARVELLAS
ESSEX HIGH SCHOOL

The Teacher-Researcher connection—We all want a scientifically literate populace!

Teachers/students have much to gain from a research experience:

- Teachers are immersed in the scientific process.
- Teachers are engaged in cutting-edge research.
- Teachers will be able to update their science content knowledge.
- Teachers will collaborate with colleagues and researchers.
- Students will "share" the experience.
- Students will experience the process of science as it is brought into the classroom.

Scientists have much to gain from working with teachers and students:

- Science education improves as teachers change to focus of their teaching.
- Scientists are exposed to new ways of thinking and teaching.

➢ **Scientists know and understand science content and the research process.**

➢ **Teachers know and understand how to translate science content and the research process into the classroom.**

The Professional Cultures of Science and Education: COMMON & UNCOMMON GROUND
Shultz, Barbara. *SEP Newsletter* Winter 1998

Scientist	Common Ground	Educator
critic	passion	nurturer
intrinsic interest in science	learning environment	cultivate interest in science
specialist	research-based	generalist
convergent questions	public mistrust/ blind faith	divergent questions
tackle simple problems 1st	prepared for the unexpected	tackle complex problems 1st
schedule from experiments	long hours	schedule from school
access to resources		limited resources
control variables		respond to variables
OK for experiments to fail		experiments can't fail

HINTS, HELPFUL SUGGESTIONS AND IMPORTANT THINGS TO REMEMBER

1. Utilize the standards (*National Science Education Standards)*—this one is critical!
2. How do you begin? Meet with teachers and teacher educators to help you plan.
3. Understand your differences and commonalities.
4. Recognize each other's strengths and weaknesses.
5. Make certain your partnership is sustainable.
6. Remember that teachers work within a constrained system and curriculum. They must be able to integrate new ideas into an existing curriculum.
7. Plan early how to assess the impact of your program.
8. Incorporate ways to "spread the wealth." Very few teachers/students can participate in an actual research experience. Those that have the opportunity must be responsible for transferring that experience and knowledge to students, other teachers and the community.

A PROGRAM THAT WORKS—TEA

Teachers Experiencing Antarctica and the Arctic (TEA) is facilitated by Rice University of Houston, TX, the Cold Regions Research and Engineering Laboratory in Hanover, NH, and the American Museum of Natural History in New York, NY. It is funded by the division of Elementary, Secondary, and Informal Education (ESIE) of the Directorate for Education and Human Resources (EHR) and the Office of Polar Programs (OPP) at the National Science Foundation (NSF).

Goals of the TEA program:

❑ To immerse teachers in a research experience as a component of their continued professional development

❑ To have research experiences inform teaching practices; science investigation in the classroom should model the scientific process and the manner in which science is conducted.

❑ To carry the polar research experience into classrooms in rich, engaging, and innovative ways that underscore the relevance of science and the scientific process to society and individuals

❑ To establish a growing collaborative "Polar Learning Community" of teachers, students, schools districts, researchers, and the community to build on the TEA experience.

Why is the TEA program so successful? (Think about the hints, helpful suggestions, and important things to remember.)

1. The program is based on the *National Science Education Standards*. Inquiry is an integral part of the standards. The Standards focus on providing inquiry-based experiences for students showing that science is a human endeavor, and underscoring the relevance of science to societal issues.

2. Teachers were involved in the planning and teachers currently serve on the advisory board.

3 and 4. The program provides teachers with the opportunity to participate in a polar research program under the guidance of a research scientist. The teacher is responsible for transferring that experience back to the classroom both during the experience (daily journals and photographs posted on the web) and after (activity development, mentoring, presenta-

tions, and participation in professional meetings). The scientist facilitates the teacher's experience, allowing her/him to become immersed in the process of science. Following the field experience, the scientist visits the teacher's classroom.

5. The field experience, while unquestionably the most exciting part of the TEA program, is still only one small piece of the teacher's commitment. Follow-up activities are an integral part of the teacher enhancement and professional development components.

6. Each TEA teacher completes two activities within two years of return from the field. These activities infuse the polar research experience into the classroom. All activities are inquiry-based and related to the *National Science Education Standards.*

7. Each TEA teacher is required to file a formal program evaluation at the close of the field season. Each year, for at least their first four years, the TEA teacher submits an annual report. The TEA teacher also collects video and print media that discusses the experience for the TEA archives.

8. Each TEA teacher is required to mentor a minimum of three peer teachers for a minimum of 140 hours each over a period of three years. In addition, each TEA teacher will create two activities, attend two professional meetings, and give at lest six presentations to the public.

Appendix F
Selected Reports on Learning from the National Academies*

Learning and Understanding: Improving Advanced Study of Mathematics and Science in U.S. High Schools Committee on Programs for Advanced Study of Mathematics and Science in American High Schools, National Research Council, 2002.

Improving Learning with Information Technology: Report of a Workshop Steering Committee on Improving Learning with Information Technology; Gail E. Pritchard, Editor; National Research Council, 2002.

Scientific Research in Education Committee on Scientific Principles for Education Research, Richard J. Shavelson and Lisa Towne, Editors, National Research Council, 2002.

Knowing What Students Know: The Science and Design of Educational Assessment Committee on the Foundations of Assessment, James W. Pellegrino, Naomi Chudowsky, and Robert Glaser, Editors, Board on Testing and Assessment, Center for Education, National Research Council, 2001.

Early Childhood Development and Learning: New Knowledge for Policy National Research Council, National Academies, 2001.

*Full text of reports available at *www.nap.edu.*

How People Learn: Brain, Mind, Experience, and School: Expanded Edition Committee on Developments in the Science of Learning with additional material from the Committee on Learning Research and Educational Practice, National Research Council, 2000.

Inquiry and the National Science Education Standards: A Guide for Teaching and Learning Steve Olson and Susan Loucks-Horsley, Editors; Committee on the Development of an Addendum to the National Science Education Standards on Scientific Inquiry, National Research Council, 2000.

How People Learn: Bridging Research and Practice M. Suzanne Donovan, John D. Bransford, and James W. Pellegrino, Editors; Committee on Learning Research and Educational Practice, National Research Council, 1999.

How People Learn: Brain, Mind, Experience, and School: Expanded Edition Committee on Developments in the Science of Learning with additional material from the Committee on Learning Research and Educational Practice, National Research Council, 2000.

Transforming Undergraduate Education in Science, Mathematics, Engineering, and Technology Committee on Undergraduate Science Education, National Research Council, 1999.